Personal Psalms

Psalms written directly to God,
directly from you,
in the present tense

Clay King

www.personalpsalms.com

Personal Psalms

www.personalpsalms.com

Second edition

ISBN: 979-8-61822-070-5

Published in Birmingham, Alabama.

Matthew 6:33   (MEV)

33 But seek first the kingdom of God and His righteousness, ...

Romans 12:1-2   (MEV)

1 I urge you therefore, brothers, by the mercies of God, that you present your bodies as a living sacrifice, holy, and acceptable to God, which is your reasonable service of worship. 2 Do not be conformed to this world, but be transformed by the renewing of your mind, that you may prove what is the good and acceptable and perfect will of God.

Table of Contents

1 - INTRODUCTION *1*

2 - A PRICELESS INVITATION *3*

*3 - ASSURANCES FROM SCRIPTURE OF YOUR
POSITION AND POSSESSIONS AS A CHILD
OF GOD* *7*

*4 - COMPARISON OF PERSONAL PSALMS
TO TRADITIONAL TRANSLATIONS OF
THE PSALMS* *13*

*5 - SUGGESTED PERSONAL PSALMS FOR
TIMES IN YOUR LIFE.* *19*

*6 - PERSONAL PSALMS
PP1 - PP150* *23*

1

<u>Introduction</u>

Welcome to Personal Psalms! This is a collection of all 150 traditional Psalms, written and meant to be read or prayed, directly to God, directly from you, in the present tense. They are written in the present tense because God is working in your life, right now; not just sometime in the future. He is not distant! He is always present in your life. As a re-born child of God, you have direct access to your Heavenly Father, to Jesus your savior, and to the Holy Spirit who lives in you. Declare your trust and confidence in Him and in His goodness and strength in your life. Read them straight through, 1-150, or choose selections from the chart of suggested Personal Psalms, for specific times in your life.

The sections to follow begin with a Priceless Invitation for anyone who has never trusted Jesus as their Savior and Lord. It may be a good reminder of your own salvation experience for those who are already saved and re-born through the death and resurrection of Jesus. The next section includes assurances from scripture of your Position and Possessions as a saved, redeemed child of God. Next, you will find a comparison of Personal Psalms to traditional translations of the Psalms to see their personal nature between you and God. You will then find a chart of suggested Personal Psalms for certain times in your life. And, finally, all 150 Personal Psalms are presented in their entirety.

Boldly claim His power, goodness, guidance, and love in your life, today and every day!

2

A Priceless Invitation

If you are reading this, but you have never accepted God's free gift of salvation, forgiveness for your sins, I pray that you will do that now. Every person who has ever lived on earth (except Jesus Christ, the Son of God) has sinned and will continue to sin until we die. God demands that we have no sin in our life if we want to spend eternity with Him in Heaven. Since none of us can achieve that standard, God offers us the free gift of forgiveness through the person of Jesus, God's only begotten Son. Jesus was conceived by the Holy Spirit (not by man), born of the Virgin Mary, and lived a sinless life on earth. He willingly gave up His life as a substitute for the penalty of your sins, my sins, and the sins of everyone who is willing to accept His sacrifice as full restitution for our sins. Innocent and sinless, Jesus was crucified, dead, on a Roman cross, and buried in a sealed tomb. As He had promised before His death, He rose from the dead on the third day, proving that He truly is the Son of God, and later ascended back into Heaven, where He sits beside God, our Heavenly Father. God declares innocent and righteous everyone who truly believes in their heart that Jesus is God's Son, accepting that His death on the cross was payment for their sins, and accepting Jesus as Lord of their life.

From Scripture:

Romans 10:9-10
New International Version (NIV)

Ro. 10:9 That if you confess with your mouth, "Jesus is Lord," and believe in your heart that God raised him from the dead, you will be saved.

Ro. 10:10 For it is with your heart that you believe and are justified, and it is with your mouth that you confess and are saved.

And

1 John 1:9
New International Version (NIV)

1Jn. 1:9 If we confess our sins, he is faithful and just and will forgive us our sins and purify us from all unrighteousness.

If you are ready to receive God's forgiveness, and all of God's goodness in your life, now and forevermore, then give your life to Him by praying this simple prayer:

Heavenly Father, I confess that I have sinned. I now repent of all my sins and turn from that life. I accept that Jesus is Your Son and that He paid my sin debt, in full. Jesus, come into my life, now. I make You my Lord and Savior.
Amen

If you genuinely prayed that prayer, all of your sins are now forgiven and the Holy Spirt has come into your life as a counselor, a guide, a protector, and as a reminder when you sin in the future (and we all continue to sin as long as we live in these sinful earthly bodies). Find a good, Bible-based church and become involved with your fellow followers of Jesus. Let them know that you have only recently given your life to Christ and are ready to begin your growth in Jesus.

Do not be discouraged or dismayed if your life does not seem to immediately change. YOU ARE immediately changed because you are a new creation in Jesus Christ.
YOU ARE A NEW CREATION, IN CHRIST, BY THE MERCY AND GRACE OF GOD!

From Scripture:

2 Corinthians 5:17
New International Version (NIV)

2Co. 5:17 Therefore, if anyone is in Christ, he is a new creation; the old has gone, the new has come!

Before we accepted Jesus as our Lord and Savior, it was impossible for us to resist the temptations of sin; we were slaves to sin. But, now, in our new life in Christ, we have the Holy Spirit living inside us, who gives us the grace to resist those old temptations. The temptation is not a sin, but when temptation to sin comes, the Holy Spirit (now in union with our own spirit) reveals to us that we are being tempted to sin. By God's grace, through the power of the Holy Spirit, we can now choose to agree with the Holy Spirit that it is sin, and immediately turn away from it, in our new life in Christ (we are no longer slaves to sin). OR, we can choose to agree with the temptation and commit the sin. Our salvation is not lost when we choose to sin after we have accepted Christ as our savior, but there are always consequences of our sins. God, because He loves us and wants to bring us into a close relationship with Himself, will often allow the consequences of our sin to affect us. He does this to bring us back to Him, turning from those sins by confessing and repenting. All of our sins (past, present, and future) were forgiven when we accepted Christ as our Lord and Savior, but God wants us to immediately confess our on-going sins, thank Him for His forgiveness that is already ours, and turn from those sins (with the help of the Holy Spirit, now living in us). This allows God to restore our relationship with Him. The peace and blessings that are ours through Christ are immediately restored with our confession to God.

Our growth in Him takes time to mature and appropriate into our daily life. Old habits and thoughts die hard, but by God's grace, our ways of thinking and acting do change. Feelings are not always truthful, but the Bible, God's Word, is always true. Don't rely on your feelings, rely on the truth and promises that God has revealed through scripture to all who have accepted Jesus as their Lord and Savior. Personal Psalms remind us of the true goodness and majesty of God, regardless of how we may feel at certain times!

Daily, spend time in prayer with God (encouraged and guided by the Holy Spirit, now living in you), and begin a daily Bible reading plan that will continue to show you how awesome is this one true God, the Creator and Sustainer of all things; God the Father, God the Son, and God the Holy Spirit.

3

Assurances from Scripture of Your Position and Possessions as a Child of God

As you read and pray these Personal Psalms back to God, you may find yourself wondering, "How can I claim these as mine?" When you accepted Jesus as your Lord and Savior, you became a new creation. You became a blessed, redeemed, forgiven, re-born, loved, accepted, approved child of the One True God. You were redeemed by the blood of Jesus, and filled with the Holy Spirit, so that God may pour out His blessings on you, allowing you to bless everyone that you encounter on your walk through life here on earth.

Below are just a few of the promises from scripture regarding your new life in Christ. The Bible is filled with hope and promises for God's children, but we must believe that He loves and cares for us so much, that He sent His only begotten Son to die for us.

John 3:16 New International Version (NIV)
16 For God so loved the world that He gave His one and only Son, that whoever believes in Him shall not perish but have eternal life.

Hebrews 4:16 New International Version (NIV)
16 Let us then approach God's throne of grace with confidence, so that we may receive mercy and find grace to help us in our time of need.

Hebrews 4:14 New International Version (NIV)

14 Therefore, since we have a great high priest who has ascended into heaven, Jesus the Son of God, let us hold firmly to the faith we profess.

Ephesians 3:12 New International Version (NIV)

12 In Him and through faith in Him we may approach God with freedom and confidence.

Romans 8:17 New International Version (NIV)

17 Now if we are children, then we are heirs—heirs of God and co-heirs with Christ, if indeed we share in His sufferings in order that we may also share in His glory.

1 Corinthians 3:21-23 New International Version (NIV)

21 So then, no more boasting about human leaders! All things are yours, 22 whether Paul or Apollos or Cephas or the world or life or death or the present or the future—all are yours, 23 and you are of Christ, and Christ is of God.

Colossians 1:16 New International Version (NIV)

16 For in Him all things were created: things in heaven and on earth, visible and invisible, whether thrones or powers or rulers or authorities; all things have been created through Him and for Him.

Galatians 3:29 New International Version (NIV)

29 If you belong to Christ, then you are Abraham's seed, and heirs according to the promise.

John 1:12-13 New International Version (NIV)

12 Yet to all who did receive Him, to those who believed in His name, He gave the right to become children of God— 13 children born not of natural descent, nor of human decision or a husband's will, but born of God.

Ephesians 1:3 New International Version (NIV)
3 Praise be to the God and Father of our Lord Jesus Christ, who has blessed us in the heavenly realms with every spiritual blessing in Christ.

Ephesians 2:6-7 New International Version (NIV)
6 And God raised us up with Christ and seated us with Him in the heavenly realms in Christ Jesus, 7 in order that in the coming ages He might show the incomparable riches of His grace, expressed in His kindness to us in Christ Jesus.

Romans 8:15 New International Version (NIV)
15 The Spirit you received does not make you slaves, so that you live in fear again; rather, the Spirit you received brought about your adoption to sonship. And by Him we cry, *"Abba, Father."*

Romans 6:6 New International Version (NIV)
6 For we know that our old self was crucified with Him so that the body ruled by sin might be done away with, that we should no longer be slaves to sin—

Galatians 4:6 New International Version (NIV)
6 Because you are His sons, God sent the Spirit of his Son into our hearts, the Spirit who calls out, *"Abba, Father."*

Ephesians 1:13 New International Version (NIV)
13 And you also were included in Christ when you heard the message of truth, the gospel of your salvation. When you believed, you were marked in Him with a seal, the promised Holy Spirit,

1 John 3:1 New International Version (NIV)
1 See what great love the Father has lavished on us, that we should be called children of God! And that is what we are! ...

Ephesians 1:4 New International Version (NIV)
4 For He chose us in Him before the creation of the world to be holy and blameless in his sight. ...

Colossians 1:22 New International Version (NIV)
22 But now He has reconciled you by Christ's physical body through death to present you holy in His sight, without blemish and free from accusation—

Romans 8:1-2 New International Version (NIV)
1 Therefore, there is now no condemnation for those who are in Christ Jesus, 2 because through Christ Jesus the law of the Spirit Who gives life has set you free from the law of sin and death.

Ephesians 1:9 New International Version (NIV)
9 He made known to us the mystery of His will according to His good pleasure, which He purposed in Christ,

Colossians 1:26 New International Version (NIV)
26 the mystery that has been kept hidden for ages and generations but is now disclosed to the Lord's people.

John 17:20-23 New International Version (NIV)
Jesus Prays for All Believers
20 "My prayer is not for them alone. I pray also for those who will believe in Me through their message, 21 that all of them may be one, Father, just as You are in Me and I am in You. May they also be in Us so that the world may believe that You have sent Me. 22 I have given them the glory that You gave Me, that they may be one as We are one— 23 I in them and You in Me—so that they may be brought to complete unity. Then the world will know that You sent Me and have loved them even as You have loved Me.

James 1:5 New International Version (NIV)
5 If any of you lacks wisdom, you should ask God, who gives generously to all without finding fault, and it will be given to you.

Luke 18:29-30 New International Version (NIV)
29 "Truly I tell you," Jesus said to them, "no one who has left home or wife or brothers or sisters or parents or children for the sake of the kingdom of God 30 will fail to receive many times as much in this age, and in the age to come eternal life."

John 14:12-14 New International Version (NIV)
12 Very truly I tell you, whoever believes in me will do the works I have been doing, and they will do even greater things than these, because I am going to the Father. 13 And I will do whatever you ask in my name, so that the Father may be glorified in the Son. 14 You may ask me for anything in my name, and I will do it.

Galatians 5:1 New International Version (NIV)
1 It is for freedom that Christ has set us free. Stand firm, then, and do not let yourselves be burdened again by a yoke of slavery.

4

Comparison of Personal Psalms to Traditional Translations of the Psalms

To help you see more clearly how Personal Psalms compare to traditional translations of the Psalms, portions of two of the most recognizable Psalms, Psalm 91 and Psalm 112, are presented side-by-side with the Personal Psalms.

Psalm 91

91 Personal Psalms (PP)	CHAPTER 91 New International Version (NIV)	Psalm 91 English Standard Version (ESV)
1 Because I dwell in Your shelter, Lord Most High, I rest in Your shadow, Lord Almighty.	Ps. 91:1 He who dwells in the shelter of the Most High will rest in the shadow of the Almighty. [Hebrew: Shaddai]	1 He who dwells in the shelter of the Most High will abide in the shadow of the Almighty.
2 I say to You, Lord, "You are my refuge and my fortress; my God, in whom I trust."	Ps. 91:2 I will say [Or He says] of the LORD, "He is my refuge and my fortress, my God, in whom I trust."	2 I will say to the Lord, "My refuge and my fortress, my God, in whom I trust."

3 You deliver me from the snare of the fowler, and from the deadly pestilence.	Ps. 91:3 Surely, he will save you from the fowler's snare and from the deadly pestilence.	3 For he will deliver you from the snare of the fowler and from the deadly pestilence.
4 You cover me with Your feathers. Under Your wings I take refuge. Your faithfulness is my shield and rampart.	Ps. 91:4 He will cover you with his feathers, and under his wings you will find refuge; his faithfulness will be your shield and rampart.	4 He will cover you with his pinions, and under his wings you will find refuge; his faithfulness is a shield and buckler.
5 I am not afraid of the terror by night, nor of the arrow that flies by day,	Ps. 91:5 You will not fear the terror of night, nor the arrow that flies by day,	5 You will not fear the terror of the night, nor the arrow that flies by day,
6 nor of the pestilence that stalks in darkness, nor of the destruction that destroys at noonday.	Ps. 91:6 nor the pestilence that stalks in the darkness, nor the plague that destroys at midday.	6 nor the pestilence that stalks in darkness, nor the destruction that wastes at noonday.
7 A thousand may fall at my side, ten thousand at my right hand, but it does not come near me.	Ps. 91:7 A thousand may fall at your side, ten thousand at your right hand, but it will not come near you.	7 A thousand may fall at your side, ten thousand at your right hand, but it will not come near you.
8 I only look with my eyes and see the punishment of the wicked.	Ps. 91:8 You will only observe with your eyes and see the punishment of the wicked.	8 You will only look with your eyes and see the recompense of the wicked.

9 Because I make You, Lord, my refuge, and You, the Most High, my dwelling place,	Ps. 91:9 If you make the Most High your dwelling — even the LORD, who is my refuge —	9 Because you have made the Lord your dwelling place— the Most High, who is my refuge—
10 no evil comes to me, neither does any plague come near my dwelling.	Ps. 91:10 then no harm will befall you, no disaster will come near your tent.	10 no evil shall be allowed to befall you, no plague come near your tent.

Psalm 112

112 Personal Psalm (PP)	CHAPTER 112 New International Version (NIV)	Psalm 112 English Standard Version (ESV)
1 Lord, I praise You! Blessed am I because I fear You and delight greatly in Your commandments.	Ps. 112:1 Praise the LORD. Blessed is the man who fears the LORD, who finds great delight in his commands.	1 Praise the Lord! Blessed is the man who fears the Lord, who greatly delights in his commandments!
2 My offspring are mighty in the land. The generation of the upright are blessed.	Ps. 112:2 His children will be mighty in the land; the generation of the upright will be blessed.	2 His offspring will be mighty in the land; the generation of the upright will be blessed.

3 Wealth and riches are in my house. My righteousness endures forever.	Ps. 112:3 Wealth and riches are in his house, and his righteousness endures forever.	3 Wealth and riches are in his house, and his righteousness endures forever.
4 Light dawns in the darkness for me because I am upright, gracious, merciful, and righteous.	Ps. 112:4 Even in darkness light dawns for the upright, for the gracious and compassionate and righteous man.	4 Light dawns in the darkness for the upright; he is gracious, merciful, and righteous.
5 It is well with me because I deal graciously and lend. I conduct my affairs with justice.	Ps. 112:5 Good will come to him who is generous and lends freely, who conducts his affairs with justice.	5 It is well with the man who deals generously and lends; conducts his affairs with justice.
6 I am never shaken. Because I am righteous, I am remembered forever.	Ps. 112:6 Surely, he will never be shaken; a righteous man will be remembered for ever.	6 For the righteous will never be moved; he will be remembered forever.
7 I am not afraid of evil news. My heart is steadfast, trusting in You, Lord.	Ps. 112:7 He will have no fear of bad news; his heart is steadfast, trusting in the LORD.	7 He is not afraid of bad news; his heart is firm, trusting in the Lord.
8 My heart is established in security. I am not afraid. In the end, I have victory over my adversaries.	Ps. 112:8 His heart is secure, he will have no fear; in the end he will look in triumph on his foes.	8 His heart is steady; he will not be afraid, until he looks in triumph on his adversaries.

9 I give widely and generously to the poor. My righteousness endures forever. My horn is exalted with honor.	Ps. 112:9 He has scattered abroad his gifts to the poor, his righteousness endures forever; his horn will be lifted high in honor.	9 He has distributed freely; he has given to the poor; his righteousness endures forever; his horn is exalted in honor.
10 The wicked see it and are grieved. They gnash their teeth and melt away. The desires of the wicked perish.	Ps. 112:10 The wicked man will see and be vexed, he will gnash his teeth and waste away; the longings of the wicked will come to nothing.	10 The wicked man sees it and is angry he gnashes his teeth and melts away; the desire of the wicked will perish!

5

Suggested Personal Psalms for Times in Your Life

Topic	Suggested Personal Psalms
Some of the most Beloved Psalms	4, 16, 18, 19, 23, 27, 30, 34, 37, 46, 51, 55, 67, 91, 94, 100, 118, 119, 139
Famous Psalms	1, 19, 22, 23, 24, 27, 30, 34, 42, 46, 47, 51, 55, 68, 84, 91, 103 111, 113, 115, 118, 119, 121, 127, 144, 150
When you need confidence that you are blessed as a child of God	1, 15, 18, 24, 25, 32, 34, 37, 40, 41, 50, 58, 61, 62, 63, 65, 66, 67, 68, 84, 85, 91, 92, 103, 106, 111, 112, 115, 125, 126, 128, 140, 144, 145, 146, 147, 149
When you need Protection	4, 16, 18, 23, 25, 27, 28, 31, 40, 46, 55, 69, 91, 94, 116, 121, 138
When you need God's strength to carry on	18, 23, 27, 28, 29, 31, 73, 89, 105, 118, 119
When you need hope	5, 9, 25, 30, 31, 33, 39, 42, 62, 71, 119, 126, 130, 143

When you need encouragement	9, 10, 16, 27, 33, 34, 37, 46, 55, 62, 91, 118, 121, 126, 145
When you need comfort from your Heavenly Father	1, 3, 6, 7, 9, 12, 13, 16, 18, 19, 22, 23, 25, 27, 28, 30, 31, 32, 33, 34, 35, 37, 38, 39, 40, 41, 43, 44, 46, 51, 54, 55, 56, 57, 59, 60, 61, 62, 64, 65, 67, 68, 69, 70, 71, 74, 75, 77, 79, 80, 83, 85, 86, 88, 90, 91, 97, 100, 102, 103, 105, 106, 107, 109, 112, 116, 118, 119, 120, 122, 123, 130, 136, 137, 138, 140, 141, 142, 143, 145, 147
When you want to praise God, or rejoice in His goodness and majesty	8, 9, 12, 13, 16, 18, 19, 20, 21, 24, 26, 27, 28, 29, 30, 32, 33, 34, 35, 36, 40, 41, 43, 44, 46, 47, 48, 50, 52, 54, 56, 57, 59, 61, 62, 63, 64, 66, 67, 68, 69, 70, 71, 72, 74, 75, 76, 77, 78, 81,86, 89, 90, 92, 93, 95, 96, 97, 98, 99, 100, 101, 102, 103, 104, 105, 106, 107, 108, 111, 112, 113, 114, 115, 116, 117, 118, 119, 134, 135, 136, 138, 139, 144, 145, 146, 147, 148, 149, 150
When you want to express your thanksgiving to God	7, 28, 30, 69, 92, 95, 100, 105, 107, 118, 136, 147
When you need to feel God's peace	4, 29, 34, 37, 46, 62, 85, 116, 119, 131

When you need inspiration	3, 33, 34, 37, 43, 46, 55, 57, 62, 67, 71, 73, 68, 69, 84, 86, 94, 100, 116, 118, 119
When you are feeling anxious or overwhelmed	4, 16, 23, 27, 34, 37, 38, 41, 44, 46, 49, 55, 56, 62, 67, 71, 73, 74, 76, 77, 80, 85, 86, 88, 89, 90, 91, 94, 96, 102, 107, 118, 128, 130, 142, 143
When you need confidence while waiting for God	25, 27, 30, 33, 34, 37, 38, 39, 40, 46, 51, 52, 59, 62, 63, 69, 72, 76, 86, 89, 104, 105, 130, 131, 135, 137, 141, 143, 145, 147, 148
When you need encouragement and confidence that you can trust God	4, 9, 14, 20, 23, 27, 29, 31, 33, 34, 36, 37, 44, 46, 47, 48, 49, 50, 52, 53, 54, 55, 56, 57, 59, 60, 61, 62, 64, 65, 66, 68, 71, 72, 74, 76, 77, 78, 81, 86, 89, 91, 93, 94, 97, 98, 100, 102, 103, 104, 105, 106, 107, 108, 111, 114, 115, 116, 117, 118, 121, 124, 125, 127, 130, 131, 132, 135, 136, 138, 140, 142, 144, 145, 147, 148

6

<u>Personal Psalms</u>

1 Blessed am I because I do not walk in the counsel of the wicked, nor stand on the path of sinners, nor sit in the seat of scoffers.

2 But my delight is in Your law, Lord. On Your law I meditate day and night.

3 I am like a tree planted by streams of water, that produces its fruit in its season, whose leaf does not wither. Whatever I do prospers.

4 The wicked are not so but are like chaff which the wind drives away.

5 Therefore the wicked shall not stand in the judgment, nor sinners in the congregation of the righteous.

6 Lord, You know my way because I am righteous before You. But You make the way of the wicked perish.

1 The nations rage, and the peoples plot in vain.

2 The kings of the earth take a stand, and the rulers take counsel together, against You, Lord, and against Your Anointed, saying,

3 "Let us break their bonds apart and cast their cords from us."

4 You sit in the heavens and laugh. You mock them.

5 Then You speak to them in Your anger, and terrify them in Your wrath, saying:

6 "I have set my King on my holy hill of Zion."

7 Lord, I tell of Your decree: You said to me, "You are my son. Today I have become Your father.

8 Ask of Me, and I will give the nations for your inheritance, the uttermost parts of the earth for your possession.

9 You shall break them with a rod of iron. You shall dash them in pieces like a potter's vessel."

10 Therefore be wise, you kings. Be instructed, you judges of the earth.

11 Serve the Lord with fear and rejoice with trembling.

12 Give sincere homage to the Son, lest He be angry, and you perish in your way, for His wrath will soon be kindled. Blessed am I because I take refuge in You, O Lord.

1 Lord, how my adversaries have increased! Many are those who rise up against me.

2 Many there are who say of me, "There is no help for him in God."

3 But You, Lord, are a shield around me, my Glory, and You lift up my head.

4 I cry to You with my voice, and You answer me out of Your holy hill.

5 I lay myself down and sleep. I awaken because You sustain me.

6 I am not afraid of tens of thousands of people who have set themselves against me on every side.

7 Lord, You arise! You save me, my God! For You strike all of my enemies on the cheek bone. You break the teeth of the wicked.

8 Salvation belongs to You. Your blessing is on Your people, of whom I am one.

1 You answer me when I call, God of my righteousness. You give me relief from my distress. You have mercy on me and hear my prayer.

2 You sons of men, how long will you dishonor my Glorious God? How Long will you love your arrogance and seek after false gods?

3 But know that the Lord Most High has set me apart for Himself because I am godly. Lord, You hear me when I call to You.

4 I am angry, but I do not sin. I search my own heart on my bed, and I am still before You.

5 I offer the sacrifices of righteousness. I put my trust in You, Lord.

6 I say, "Who will show me any good?" Lord, You let the light of Your face shine on me.

7 You put gladness in my heart; more than when their grain and their new wine are increased.

8 In peace I lay myself down and sleep, for You alone, O Lord, make me live in safety.

1 Lord, You give ear to my words, and You consider my meditation.

2 You listen to the voice of my cry, my King and my God, for I pray to You.

3 In the morning You hear my voice. In the morning I lay my requests before You and watch expectantly.

4 For You are not a God who has pleasure in wickedness. Evil cannot live with You.

5 The arrogant do not stand in Your sight. You hate all workers of iniquity.

6 You destroy those who speak lies. You abhor the bloodthirsty and deceitful man.

7 But as for me, in the abundance of Your loving kindness, I come into Your house. I bow toward Your holy temple in reverence of You.

8 You lead me in Your righteousness because of my enemies. You make Your way straight before my face.

9 For there is no faithfulness in their mouth. Their heart is destruction. Their throat is an open tomb. They flatter with their tongue.

10 But, God, You hold them guilty. You let them fall by their own plans. You thrust them out into the darkness because of the multitude of their transgressions, for they rebel against You.

11 But because I take refuge in You, I rejoice. I always shout for joy and I am joyful in You because You defend me.

12 You bless me because I am righteous. Lord, you surround me with favor as with a shield.

PP 6 PP 6

1 Lord, You do not rebuke me in Your anger, neither do You discipline me in Your wrath.

2 You have mercy on me for I am faint. You heal me, for my bones are troubled.

3 My soul is also in great anguish. How long, Lord—how long?

4 Still, You return and deliver my soul. You save me for Your loving kindness' sake.

5 For in death there is no memory of You. In the grave, no one gives You praise.

6 I am weary with my groaning. Every night I flood my bed. I drench my couch with my tears.

7 My eyes waste away because of my grief. I grow old because of all my adversaries.

8 Lord, because You hear the voice of my weeping, all the workers of iniquity depart from me.

9 You hear my requests for mercy. You accept my prayer.

10 All my enemies are ashamed and dismayed. They turn back and are disgraced suddenly because of You.

1 Lord, my God, I take refuge in You. You save me from all those who pursue me, and You deliver me,

2 lest they tear apart my soul like a lion, ripping it in pieces, while there is no one to deliver me.

3 Lord, my God, if I have done this, if there is iniquity in my hands,

4 if I have rewarded evil to him who was at peace with me,

5 let the enemy pursue my soul, and overtake it; yes, let him tread my life down to the earth, and lay my glory in the dust.

6 But, Lord, You arise in your anger. You lift Yourself up against the rage of my adversaries. You awaken for me. You command Your judgment.

7 You let the congregation of the peoples surround You. You rule over them from on high.

8 You administer judgment to the peoples. You judge me according to my righteousness, and my integrity that is in me.

9 You bring the wickedness of the wicked to an end but establish me because I am righteous; my mind and heart are searched by You, the righteous God.

10 My shield is with You, God; You save me because I am upright in heart.

11 You are a righteous judge; yes, a God who shows Your righteous anger every day.

12 If a man does not repent, You sharpen Your sword; You bend and string Your bow.

13 You prepare for Yourself the instruments of death. You make ready Your flaming arrows.

14 You take notice of he who lives with wickedness. Yes, he conceives mischief, and gives birth to discouragement.

15 He digs a hole, but he, himself, falls into the pit which he made.

16 You bring the trouble that he causes back to his own head. His violence comes down on the crown of his own head.

17 I give thanks to You because of Your righteousness, and sing praise to Your name, Lord Most High.

PP 8 —————◆————— PP 8

1 O Lord, my Lord, how majestic is Your name in all the earth! You set Your glory above the heavens!

2 Even the lips of children and infants praise You, because of Your adversaries, that You might silence the enemy and the avenger.

3 When I consider Your heavens, the work of Your fingers, the moon and the stars, which You ordained,

4 what am I, a man, that You think of me? What am I that You care for me?

5 Still, You made me a little lower than the angels and crowned me with glory and honor.

6 You make me ruler over the works of Your hands. You put all things under my feet:

7 All sheep and cattle, yes, and the animals of the field,

8 the birds of the sky, the fish of the sea, and whatever passes through the paths of the seas.

9 Lord, my Lord, how majestic is Your name in all the earth!

PP 9 PP 9

1 Lord, I give You thanks with my whole heart. I tell of all Your marvelous works.

2 I am glad and rejoice in You. I sing praise to Your name, O Most High.

3 My enemies turn back; they stumble and perish in Your presence.

4 For You maintain my just cause. You sit on Your throne judging righteously.

5 You rebuke the nations. You destroy the wicked. You blot out their name forever and ever.

6 The enemy is overtaken by endless ruin. The very memory of the cities which You have overthrown perishes.

7 But You, Lord, reign forever. You prepare Your throne for judgment.

8 You judge the world in righteousness. You administer judgment to the peoples in uprightness.

9 You are a high tower for me because I am oppressed; a high tower in times of trouble.

10 Because I know Your name, I put my trust in You. You do not forsake me because I seek You.

11 I sing praises to You, who dwell in Zion, and I declare among the people Your magnificent works.

12 For You avenge my blood and remember me. You do not forget my cry when I am afflicted.

13 You have mercy on me, Lord. You see my affliction by those who hate me, and lift me up from the gates of death,

14 that I may speak loudly of Your praise. I rejoice in Your salvation in the gates of the daughter of Zion.

15 The nations sink down in the pit that they made. In the net which they hid, their own foot is snared.

16 Lord, You make Yourself known. You execute judgment. The wicked are snared by the work of their own hands.

17 You turn the wicked back to the grave, even all the nations that forget You, God.

18 Because I am needy, You do not forget me, nor do You let my hope perish forever because I am poor.

19 You arise, O Lord! You do not let man prevail. You judge the nations in Your presence.

20 You put them in fear. You let the nations know that they are only men.

1 Why do You stand far off, Lord? Why do You hide Yourself in times of trouble?

2 In arrogance, the wicked hunt me down because I am weak. I am caught in the schemes that they devise.

3 For the wicked boasts of his heart's cravings. He blesses the greedy and condemns You, Lord.

4 The wicked, in his pride, has no room in his thoughts for You.

5 His ways are prosperous at all times. He is arrogant, and Your laws are far from his sight. As for all his adversaries, he sneers at them.

6 He says in his heart, "I shall not be shaken. For generations I shall have no trouble."

7 His mouth is full of cursing, deceit, and oppression. Under his tongue is mischief and iniquity.

8 He lies in wait near the villages. From ambushes, he murders the innocent. His eyes are secretly set against the helpless.

9 He lurks in secret as a lion in his ambush. He lies in wait to catch me. He catches me when I am helpless and draws me into his net.

10 I am crushed because I am helpless. I collapse. I fall under his strength.

11 He says about me in his heart, "God has forgotten and hides His face. He will never see it."

12 But You arise, O Lord! You lift up Your hand! You do not forget me.

13 The wicked person condemns You and says in his heart, "God will not call me into account."

14 But You do see trouble and grief. You consider it and take it into Your hand. You help me, as You help the victim and the fatherless.

15 You break the arm of the wicked. As for the evil man, You seek out his wickedness that he thought would not be found out.

16 Lord, You are King forever and ever! The nations will perish out of Your land.

17 You hear my desires because I am humble before You. You encourage my heart and listen to my plea

18 to defend the fatherless and the oppressed, so that man, who is of the earth, may terrify no more.

PP 11 PP 11

1 Lord, in You I take refuge. How can You say to my soul, "Flee as a bird to your mountain"?

2 For, behold, the wicked bend their bows. They set their arrows on the strings, that they may shoot in darkness at me because I am upright in heart.

3 If the foundations are destroyed, what can the righteous do?

4 Still, You are in Your holy temple, Lord. You are on Your throne in heaven. Your eyes observe. Your eyes examine the children of men.

5 You, Lord, the Righteous One, examine the wicked, and Your soul hates those who love violence.

6 On the wicked, You rain blazing coals; fire, sulfur, and scorching wind are the portion of their cup.

7 For You, Lord, are righteous. You love righteousness. Because I am upright, I see Your face.

PP 12

PP 12

1 Lord, You help me because godly men have disappeared. The faithful disappear from among the children of men.

2 Everyone lies to his neighbor. They speak with flattering lips, and deception.

3 But You cut off all flattering lips and tongues that boast;

4 those evildoers who say, "With our tongue we will prevail. Our lips are our own. Who is lord over us?"

5 Lord, You say, "Because of the oppression of the weak and because of the groaning of the needy, I now arise, and I protect you from those who malign you."

6 Lord, Your words are flawless words, like silver refined in a clay furnace, purified seven times.

7 You keep me safe. You protect me from this generation forever.

8 The wicked walk about proudly when what is vile is honored among the sons of men.

PP 13 PP 13

1 How long, O Lord? Will You forget me forever? How long will You hide Your face from me?

2 How long shall I wrestle in my soul, having sorrow in my heart every day? How long shall my enemy triumph over me?

3 But You look on me, and answer me, O Lord, my God. You give light to my eyes, or I would sleep in death.

4 My enemies would say, "We have prevailed against him." My adversaries would rejoice when I fall.

5 But I trust in Your loving kindness. My heart rejoices in Your salvation.

6 Lord, I sing to You because You are good to me.

1 The fool says in his heart, "There is no God." They are corrupt. They do abominable deeds. There is no one who does good.

2 Lord, You look down from heaven on the children of men, to see if there are any who understand; any who seek after You.

3 They have all gone astray. They have together become corrupt. There is no one who does good, no, not one.

4 All the workers of iniquity never learn. They eat up Your people as men eat bread, and they do not call on You, Lord.

5 But they are in great fear, because You, God, are with me, because I am righteous before You.

6 Evildoers frustrate my plan because I am poor, but You, Lord, are my refuge.

7 Oh that the salvation of Israel would come out of Zion! When You, Lord, restore the fortunes of Your people, then Jacob shall rejoice, and Israel shall be glad.

1 Lord, I dwell in Your sanctuary and live on Your holy hill

2 because I walk blamelessly before You and do what is right. I speak truth in my heart.

3 I do not slander with my tongue, nor do evil to my friend, nor cast slurs against my fellow man.

4 I despise a vile man, but I honor those who fear You, Lord. I keep an oath even when it hurts, and I do not change.

5 I do not lend out money for usury, nor take a bribe against the innocent. Because I do these things, I am never shaken.

PP 16 PP 16

1 God, You preserve me, and I take refuge in You.

2 My soul, says to You, "You are my Lord. Apart from You I have no good thing."

3 As for the saints who are on the earth, they are the excellent ones in whom is all my delight.

4 Their sorrows are increased who give gifts to another god. Their drink offerings of blood I will not offer, nor take their names on my lips.

5 Lord, You assign my portion and my cup. You make my lot secure.

6 The lines fall to me in pleasant places. Yes, I have a good inheritance.

7 I bless You, Lord, because You give me counsel. Yes, my heart instructs me in the night.

8 I set You always before me. Because You are at my right hand, I am not moved.

9 Therefore my heart is glad, and my tongue rejoices. My body dwells in safety.

10 For You do not leave my soul in the grave, neither do You allow your Holy One to see corruption.

11 You show me the path of life. In Your presence is fullness of joy. In Your right hand there are pleasures forever more.

PP 17 PP 17

1 Lord, You hear my righteous plea. You give ear to my prayer that does not come out of deceitful lips.

2 You vindicate me in Your presence. Your eyes look on my righteousness.

3 You prove my heart. You visit me in the night. You have tried me and found nothing. I resolve that my mouth shall not disobey.

4 As for the deeds of men, by the word of Your lips, I keep myself from the ways of the violent.

5 My steps hold fast to Your paths. My feet do not slip.

6 I call on You, and You answer me. You turn your ear to me. You hear my prayer.

7 You show me Your marvelous loving kindness. You save me by Your right hand because I take refuge in You from my enemies.

8 You keep me as the apple of Your eye. You hide me under the shadow of Your wings

9 from the wicked who oppress me; my deadly enemies who surround me.

10 They close up their callous hearts. With their mouth they speak proudly.

11 They found me and surrounded me in my steps. They set their eyes to cast me down to the earth.

12 They are like a lion that desires his prey; as it were, a strong lion lurking in secret places.

13 Lord, You arise and confront them. You cast them down. You deliver my soul from the wicked by Your sword.

14 By Your hand You deliver me from men of the world, whose portion is in this life. You fill my belly because I am one of Your cherished ones. I have plenty because I am one of Your sons, and You store up wealth for my children.

15 In righteousness, I see Your face. I am satisfied, when I awake, with seeing You.

PP 18 PP 18

1 I love You, Lord. You are my strength.

2 You are my rock, my fortress, and my deliverer; my God, my rock, in whom I take refuge; my shield, and the horn of my salvation, my high tower.

3 I call on You because You are worthy to be praised, and You save me from my enemies.

4 The cords of death surrounded me. The floods of ungodliness made me afraid.

5 The cords of the grave were around me. The snares of death came on me.

6 In my distress I called to You and cried to You, my God. You heard my voice out of Your temple. My cry before You came into Your ears.

7 Then the earth shook and trembled. The foundations also of the mountains quaked and were shaken, because You were angry.

8 Smoke went out of Your nostrils. Consuming fire came out of Your mouth. Coals were kindled by it.

9 You opened the heavens and came down. Thick darkness was under Your feet.

10 You ride on a cherub and fly. Yes, You soar on the wings of the wind.

11 You make darkness Your hiding place, Your pavilion around You; thick clouds of the skies.

12 From Your brightness before You, thick clouds pass with hailstones and coals of fire.

13 You thunder in the sky. You, the Most High, utter Your voice with hailstones and coals of fire.

14 You send out Your arrows and scatter the enemies. You rout them with great lightning bolts.

15 The channels of waters appear. The foundations of the world are laid bare at Your rebuke, Lord; at the blast of the breath of Your nostrils.

16 You reach from on high and take me. You draw me out of deep waters.

17 You deliver me from my strong enemies, from those who hate me; for they are too mighty for me.

18 They come on me in the day of my calamity, but You, Lord, are my support.

19 You bring me out into a large place. You deliver me, because You delight in me.

20 You reward me because of my righteousness before You; according to the cleanness of my hands. You reward me

21 for I keep Your ways and do not wickedly depart from You.

22 For all Your ordinances are before me. I do not put away Your statutes from before me.

23 I am blameless before You. I keep myself from iniquity.

24 Therefore You reward me according to my righteousness, according to the cleanness of my hands in Your sight.

25 To the merciful You show Yourself merciful. To the righteous, You show Yourself righteous.

26 To the pure, You show Yourself pure. But, to the crooked You show Yourself shrewd.

27 You save me because I am afflicted, but the arrogant You bring down.

28 For You light my lamp, Lord. My God, You light up my darkness.

29 For by You, I advance through a troop. By You, my God, I leap over a wall.

30 As for You, God, Your way is perfect. Your word is perfect. You are a shield to me, and I take refuge in You.

31 For who is God, except You? Who is a rock, besides You, my God?

32 You arm me with strength and make my way perfect.

33 You make my feet like deer's feet and set me on high places.

34 You teach my hands to be successful in battle, so that my arms bend a bow of bronze.

35 You give me the shield of your salvation. Your right hand sustains me. In Your kindness and gentleness, You make me great.

36 You widen the path under me, My feet do not slip.

37 I pursue my enemies and overtake them. I do not turn away until they are consumed.

38 I strike them through, so that they are not able to rise. They fall under my feet.

39 You arm me with strength for the battle. You subdue under me those who rise up against me.

40 You make my enemies turn their backs to me, that I might cut off those who hate me.

41 They cry, but there is no one to save them. They cry even to You, but You do not answer them.

42 Then I beat them as small as the dust before the wind. I cast them out as the mire of the streets.

43 You deliver me from the attacks of the people. You make me the head of the nations. A people whom I have not known serve me.

44 As soon as they hear of me, they obey me. Foreigners submit themselves to me.

45 The foreigners lose courage and come trembling out of their strongholds.

46 Lord, You live! Blessed are You, my Rock. Exalted are You, the God of my salvation.

47 You are the God who executes vengeance for me and subdues peoples under me.

48 You rescue me from my enemies. Yes, You lift me up above those who rise up against me. You deliver me from the violent man.

49 Therefore I give thanks to You, Lord, among the nations, and sing praises to Your name.

50 You give great deliverance and show loving kindness to me, as You did for Your anointed, to David and to his descendants, forever more.

1 God, the heavens declare Your glory. The skies show Your handiwork.

2 Day after day the heavens pour out speech, and night after night they display knowledge.

3 There is no speech nor language where their voice is not heard.

4 Their voice has gone out through all the earth, their words to the end of the world. In them You have set a tent for the sun,

5 which is as a bridegroom coming out of his room, like a strong man rejoicing to run his course.

6 Its going out is from one end of the heavens to the other end. There is nothing hidden from its heat.

7 Your law, O Lord, is perfect, restoring the soul. Your covenant is trustworthy, making wise the simple.

8 Your teachings are right, rejoicing the heart. Your commandments are pure, enlightening the eyes.

9 The fear of You is pure, enduring forever. Your ordinances are true, and righteous altogether.

10 They are more to be desired than gold, yes, than much fine gold; sweeter than honey and the extract of the honeycomb.

11 I am warned by them. In keeping them, I receive great reward.

12 Who can discern my errors? Lord, You forgive me from my hidden errors.

13 You keep me also from willful sins. You do not let them have dominion over me. I am upright. I am blameless and innocent of great transgression.

14 Let the words of my mouth and the meditation of my heart be acceptable in Your sight, O Lord, my rock, and my redeemer.

PP 20 — PP 20

1 Lord, You answer me in my day of trouble. Your name, the name of the God of Jacob, sets me up on high.

2 You send me help from Your sanctuary; You grant me support from Zion.

3 You remember all my offerings and accept my burned sacrifice.

4 You grant me my heart's desire and make all my plans succeed.

5 I shout joyfully in Your salvation. In Your name, God, I set up my banners. You, Lord, grant all my requests.

6 Now I know that You save me, Your anointed. You answer me from Your holy heaven, with the saving strength of Your right hand.

7 Some trust in chariots, and some in horses, but I trust in Your name, the Lord my God.

8 My enemies are brought down and fallen, but I rise up, and stand upright.

9 You save me, Lord! You answer me when I call!

PP 21

PP 21

1 Lord, I rejoice in Your strength! How greatly I rejoice in Your salvation!

2 You give me my heart's desire, and You do not withhold the request of my lips.

3 You meet me with blessings of goodness. You set a crown of fine gold on my head.

4 I ask life of You and You give it to me; even length of days forever and ever.

5 My glory is great in Your salvation. You lay honor and majesty on me.

6 You make me most blessed forever. You make me glad with joy in Your presence.

7 For I trust in You, Lord. Through Your loving kindness, Lord Most High, I am not moved.

8 Your hand finds out all of Your enemies. Your right hand takes hold of those who hate You.

9 You make them as a fiery furnace in the time of Your anger. You swallow them up in Your wrath. Your fire devours them.

10 You destroy their descendants from the earth; their posterity from among the children of men.

11 For they intend evil against You. They plot evil against You which does not succeed.

12 For You make them turn their back, when You aim Your drawn bow at their face.

13 Lord, I exalt You in Your strength. I sing and praise Your power.

 PP 22

1 My God, my God, why have You forsaken me? Why are You so far from helping me, and from the words of my groaning?

2 My God, I cry in the daytime, but You do not answer; in the night, I am not silent.

3 But You are holy. You inhabit the praises of Israel.

4 My fathers trusted in You. They trusted, and You delivered them.

5 They cried to You and were delivered. They trusted in You and were not disappointed.

6 But I am a worm, not a man; a reproach of men, and despised by the people.

7 All those who see me mock me. They insult me with their lips. They shake their heads, saying,

8 "He trusts in the Lord. Let the Lord deliver him. Let the Lord rescue him, since he delights in the Lord God."

9 But You brought me out of the womb. You made me trust You while at my mother's breasts.

10 I was thrown on You from my mother's womb. You have been my God since before my mother bore me.

11 Lord, You are not far from me, although trouble is near, and there is no one to help me.

12 Many bulls surround me. Strong bulls of Bashan encircle me.

13 They open their mouths wide against me, like lions tearing prey and roaring.

14 I am poured out like water. All my bones are out of joint. My heart is like wax. It melts within me.

15 My strength is dried up like a potsherd. My tongue sticks to the roof of my mouth. You bring me into the dust of death.

16 For dogs surround me. A company of evildoers enclose me. They pierce my hands and feet.

17 I can count all of my bones. They look and stare at me.

18 They divide my garments among them. They cast lots for my clothing.

19 But You are not far off, Lord. You are my help. You hurry to help me!

20 You deliver my soul from the sword, my precious life from the power of the dog.

21 You save me from the lion's mouth! Yes, You rescue me from the horns of the wild oxen.

22 I declare Your name to my brothers. Among the assembly, I praise You.

23 Because I fear You, Lord, I praise You! All you descendants of Jacob, glorify the Lord! Stand in awe of Him, all you descendants of Israel!

24 Lord, You do not despise nor abhor my suffering when I am afflicted. Neither do You hide Your face from me. But when I cry to You, You hear me.

25 I praise You in the great assembly. I fulfill my vows before those who fear You.

26 Because I am humble before You, Lord, I eat, and I am satisfied. I praise You as I seek after You. My heart lives forever.

27 All the ends of the earth remember and turn to You, Lord. All the relatives of the nations worship before You.

28 For the kingdom is Yours. You are the ruler over all the nations.

29 All the rich ones of the earth eat and worship. All those who go down to the dust bow before You; all who cannot keep themselves alive.

30 Posterity will serve You. Future generations shall be told about You, Lord.

31 They shall come and declare Your righteousness to a people yet to be born, for You have done it.

PP 23

1 Lord, You are my shepherd; I lack nothing.

2 You make me lie down in green pastures. You lead me beside still waters.

3 You restore my soul. You guide me in the paths of righteousness for Your name's sake.

4 Even though I walk through the valley of the shadow of death, I fear no evil, for You are with me. Your rod and Your staff, they comfort me.

5 You prepare a table before me in the presence of my enemies. You anoint my head with oil. My cup runs over.

6 Surely goodness and loving kindness follow me all the days of my life, and I will dwell in Your house forever, O Lord.

PP 24 PP 24

1 Lord, the earth is Yours with all its fullness; the world, and all those who dwell in it.

2 For You founded it on the seas and established it on the floods.

3 Who may ascend to Your hill? Who may stand in Your holy place?

4 Because I have clean hands and a pure heart, because I have not lifted up my soul to falsehood, and have not sworn deceitfully,

5 I am blessed by You. I receive righteousness from You, God of my salvation.

6 This is the generation of those who seek You, who seek Your face—Lord, God of Jacob.

7 Lift up your heads, you gates! Be lifted up, you everlasting doors, and the King of Glory comes in.

8 Who is this King of Glory? You, Lord, strong and mighty. You are mighty in battle.

9 Lift up your heads, you gates, yes, lift them up, you everlasting doors, and the King of Glory comes in.

10 Who is this King of Glory? You, the Lord Almighty, are the King of Glory!

PP 25 PP 25

1 To You, O Lord, I lift up my soul.

2 My God, I trust in You. You do not let me be shamed. You do not let my enemies triumph over me.

3 Because I wait for You, I am not shamed. But You shame those who deal treacherously with me without cause.

4 You show me Your ways, Lord. You teach me Your paths.

5 You guide me in Your truth, and teach me, for You are the God of my salvation. I wait for You all day long.

6 You remember Your tender mercies and Your loving kindness, for they are from old times.

7 You do not remember the sins of my youth, nor my transgressions. You remember me according to Your loving kindness, for Your goodness' sake, Lord.

8 You are good and upright. You instruct sinners in Your way.

9 You guide me in justice because I am humble before You. You teach the humble Your way.

10 All of Your paths are loving kindness and truth to me because I keep Your covenant and Your testimonies.

11 For Your name's sake, You pardon my iniquity, although it is great.

12 Because I fear You, You instruct me in the way that I choose.

13 My soul dwells at ease. My offspring inherit the land.

14 Your friendship, Lord, is with me because I fear You. You show me Your covenant.

15 My eyes are ever on You and You pluck my feet out of the net.

16 You turn to me and have mercy on me because I am desolate and afflicted.

17 The troubles of my heart are enlarged, but You bring me out of my distresses.

18 You consider my affliction and my travail. You forgive all my sins.

19 You consider my enemies, for they are many. They hate me with cruel hatred.

20 But You guard my life and deliver me. I am not disappointed, for I take refuge in You.

21 My integrity and uprightness preserve me, as I wait for You.

22 God, You redeem me, along with Your people, Israel, out of all my troubles!

PP 26 PP 26

1 Lord, You defend me for I walk in integrity before You. I trust You without wavering.

2 You examine me and test me. You try my heart and my mind.

3 Your loving kindness is before my eyes. I walk in Your truth.

4 I do not sit with deceitful men, neither do I go in with hypocrites.

5 I hate the assembly of evildoers and do not sit with the wicked.

6 I wash my hands in innocence so I may go about Your altar, Lord.

7 I make my voice of thanksgiving heard and tell of all Your wondrous deeds.

8 Lord, I love Your house, the place where Your glory dwells.

9 You do not gather my soul with sinners, nor my life with bloodthirsty men

10 in whose hands is wickedness; their right hand is full of bribes.

11 But as for me, I walk in integrity before You. You redeem me and are merciful to me.

12 My feet stand on a level place. In the congregations I praise You, Lord.

PP 27

PP 27

1 Lord, You are my light and my salvation, therefore, I fear no one. You are the strength of my life; therefore, I am afraid of no one.

2 When evildoers come at me to eat up my flesh, even my adversaries and my foes, they stumble and fall.

3 Though an army encamps against me, my heart does not fear. Though war rises against me, even then I am confident.

4 One thing I ask of You, Lord, one thing I desire: that I may dwell in Your house all the days of my life, to see Your beauty and to inquire in Your temple.

5 For in the day of trouble, You keep me secretly in Your pavilion. In the secret place of Your tabernacle, You hide me. You lift me up on a rock.

6 You lift up my head above my enemies around me. I offer sacrifices of joy in Your tent. I sing, yes, I sing praises to You, Lord.

7 You hear when I cry with my voice. You have mercy on me and answer me.

8 When You say, "Seek my face," my heart says to You, "I seek Your face, O Lord."

9 You do not hide Your face from me. You do not put Your servant away in anger. You, God of my salvation, are my help. You do not abandon me, neither do You forsake me.

10 When my father and my mother forsake me, then, Lord, You take me up.

11 You teach me Your way. You lead me in a straight path, because of my enemies.

12 You do not deliver me over to the desire of my adversaries, for false witnesses rise up against me, and breathe out cruelty.

13 I am confident of this: I will always see Your goodness, Lord, in the land of the living.

14 I wait for You. I am strong, and my heart takes courage as I wait for You, Lord.

1 Lord, I call to You. God, my Rock, You are not deaf to me. If You were silent to me, I would become like those who go down into the pit.

2 You hear the voice of my petitions when I cry to You, when I lift up my hands toward Your most holy place.

3 You do not draw me away with the wicked, with the workers of iniquity who speak peace with their neighbors, but mischief is in their hearts.

4 You give to them according to their work, and according to the wickedness of their deeds. You give to them according to the workings of their hands. You bring back on them what they deserve.

5 Because they do not respect Your works, Lord, nor the accomplishments of Your hands, You break them down and never build them up again.

6 Blessed are You because You hear my petitions.

7 You are my strength and my shield. My heart trusts in You, and I am helped. My heart greatly rejoices. With my song I thank You.

8 Lord, You are my strength. You are my stronghold of salvation because I am one of Your anointed.

9 You save me, along with all Your people, and bless Your inheritance. You are my shepherd, and You bear me up forever.

PP 29 PP 29

1 I ascribe to You glory and strength, Lord; the sons of the mighty ascribe to You glory and strength.

2 I ascribe to You the glory due Your name. I worship You in Your holy splendor.

3 Your voice is on the waters. You, the God of Glory, thunder on strong waters.

4 Your voice is powerful. Your voice is full of majesty.

5 Your voice breaks the cedars. Yes, You break in pieces the cedars of Lebanon.

6 You make Lebanon to skip like a calf; and Sirion like a young, wild ox.

7 Your voice strikes with flashes of lightning.

8 Your voice shakes the wilderness. You shake the wilderness of Kadesh.

9 Your voice makes the deer calve and strips the forests bare. In Your temple everything says, "Glory!"

10 You sit enthroned at the flood. Yes, You, Lord, sit as King forever.

11 You give strength to me and all Your people. You bless Your people with peace.

PP 30   PP 30

1 Lord, I exalt You for You raise me up, and You do not allow my foes to rejoice over me.

2 Lord, my God, I cry to You, and You heal me.

3 You bring my soul up from the grave. You keep me alive, so that I do not go down to the pit.

4 With all Your saints, I sing praise to You. I give thanks to Your holy name.

5 For Your anger is only for a moment, but Your favor is for a lifetime. Weeping may stay for the night, but joy comes in the morning.

6 As for me, I say in my prosperity, "I am never moved."

7 Because You favor me, Lord, my mountain stands strong; but if You hide Your face, I am troubled.

8 I cry to You. I make supplication to You:

9 "What profit is there in my destruction, if I go down to the pit? Shall the dust praise You? Shall the dust declare Your truth?

10 Lord, You hear me, and You have mercy on me. You are my helper."

11 You turn my mourning into dancing for me. You remove my sackcloth, and clothe me with gladness,

12 so that my heart sings praise to You and is not silent. Lord my God, I give thanks to You forever!

PP 31 PP 31

1 Lord, I take refuge in You. You never let me be shamed. You deliver me in Your righteousness.

2 You bow down Your ear to me. You deliver me speedily. You are to me a strong rock; a house of defense that saves me.

3 Because You are my rock and my fortress, You lead me and guide me, for Your name's sake.

4 You pluck me out of the net that my enemies laid secretly for me, for You are my refuge.

5 Into Your hand I commend my spirit. You redeem me Lord, God of truth.

6 I hate those who regard worthless idols, but I trust in You, Lord.

7 I am glad and rejoice in Your loving kindness, for You see my affliction. You know me in my adversities.

8 You have not shut me up into the hand of my enemy. You have set my feet in a large place.

9 You have mercy on me, Lord, for I am in distress. My eyes, my soul, and my body waste away with grief.

10 My life is spent with sorrow, my years with sighing. My strength fails because of my iniquity. My bones waste away.

11 Because of all my adversaries I have become utterly contemptible to my neighbors; a horror to my acquaintances. Those who see me on the street flee from me.

12 I am forgotten from their hearts like a dead man. I am like broken pottery.

13 For I hear the slander of many, terror on every side, while they conspire together against me. They plot to take away my life.

14 But I trust in You, Lord. I say, "You are my God."

15 My times are in Your hand. You deliver me from the hand of my enemies and from those who persecute me.

16 You make Your face to shine on me, Your servant. You save me in Your loving kindness.

17 I am not ashamed for I call on You. But You shame the wicked and let them be silent in the grave.

18 You make the lying lips be mute, which speak against the righteous insolently, with pride and contempt.

19 Oh how great is Your goodness, which You laid up for me because I fear You; which You work for me because I take refuge in You, before the sons of men!

20 In the shelter of Your presence, You hide me from the plotting of man. You keep me secretly in Your dwelling, away from my accusers.

21 I praise You, Lord, for You show me Your marvelous loving kindness in a strong city.

22 As for me, I said in my haste, "I am cut off from before Your eyes." But You hear the voice of my petitions when I cry to You.

23 Oh, I love You, Lord. I am one of Your saints! You preserve me because I am faithful. You fully pay back him who behaves arrogantly.

24 Along with all who hope in You, I am strong, and my heart takes courage.

PP 32 PP 32

1 Blessed am I because You forgive my disobedience; my sin is covered.

2 Lord, blessed am I because You do not impute iniquity to me. In my spirit there is no deceit.

3 When I keep silent, my bones waste away through my groaning all day long.

4 For in those days, day and night Your hand is heavy on me. My strength is sapped like in the heat of summer.

5 But, I acknowledge my sin to You. I do not hide my iniquity. I confess my transgressions to You, Lord, and You forgive the iniquity of my sin.

6 I pray to You, with everyone who is godly, in a time when You may be found. Surely when the great waters overflow, they do not reach me.

7 You are my hiding place. You preserve me from trouble. You surround me with songs of deliverance.

8 You instruct me and teach me in the way which I shall go. You counsel me with Your eye on me.

9 I am not like the horse, or like the mule, which have no understanding; who are controlled by bit and bridle, or else they will not come near to You.

10 Many sorrows come to the wicked, but loving kindness surrounds me and all who trust in You.

11 I am glad in You, Lord, and I rejoice with all the righteous! I shout for joy, with all who are upright in heart!

1 Lord, with all the righteous, I rejoice in You! Praise to You is fitting for the upright.

2 I give thanks to You with the lyre and sing praises to You with the harp of ten strings.

3 I sing to You a new song, and I play skillfully with a shout of joy!

4 For Your word is right. All Your work is done in faithfulness.

5 You love righteousness and justice. The earth is full of Your loving kindness.

6 By Your word the heavens were made; all the stars were made by the breath of Your mouth.

7 You gather the waters of the sea together as a heap. You lay up the deeps in storehouses.

8 With all the earth, I fear You, Lord. With all the inhabitants of the world, I stand in awe of You.

9 For You spoke, and it was done. You commanded, and creation stood firm.

10 You bring the plans of the nations to nothing. You make the thoughts of the peoples to be of no effect.

11 Lord, Your plans stand fast forever; the thoughts of Your heart to all generations.

12 Blessed is the nation whose God is You, Lord; the people whom You have chosen for Your own inheritance.

13 You look from heaven. You see all the sons of men.

14 From Your place of habitation, You look out on all the inhabitants of the earth.

15 You fashion their hearts and consider all of their works.

16 There is no king saved by the multitude of an army. A mighty man is not delivered by great strength.

17 A horse is hopeless for safety, neither does it deliver anyone by its great power.

18 Behold, Your eye is on me because I fear You and hope in Your loving kindness,

19 to deliver my soul from death and keep me alive in famine.

20 My soul waits in hope for You. You are my help and my shield.

21 My heart rejoices in You, because I trust in Your holy name.

22 Lord, Your loving kindness is on me since my hope is in You.

PP 34 PP 34

1 Lord, I bless You at all times. Your praise is always in my mouth.

2 My soul boasts in You. The humble hear of it and are glad.

3 With me, all the people magnify You, Lord. We exalt Your name.

4 I seek You and You answer me. You deliver me from all my fears.

5 I look to You and I am radiant. My face is never covered with shame.

6 I am a poor man. I cry to You and You hear me. You save me out of all my troubles.

7 Your angel encamps around me and You deliver me because I fear You.

8 Oh, I taste, and I see that You are good. Blessed am I because I take refuge in You.

9 With all Your saints, I fear You. I lack nothing because I fear You.

10 The young lions suffer lack and hunger. But I lack no good thing because I seek You.

11 Come, you children, listen to me. I will teach you the fear of the Lord.

12 Because I desire life, and love to see many good days,

13 I keep my tongue from evil, and my lips from speaking lies.

14 I depart from evil and I do good. I seek peace and pursue it.

15 Your eyes are toward me because I am righteous. Your ears hear my cry.

16 Your face is against those who do evil. You cut off their memory from the earth.

17 I cry out and You hear me because I am righteous before You. You deliver me out of all my troubles.

18 You are near to me when I have a broken heart. You save me when I have a crushed spirit.

19 Many are my afflictions even though I am righteous, but You, Lord, deliver me out of them all.

20 You protect all of my bones. Not one of them is broken.

21 The wicked are killed by evil. Those who hate the righteous are condemned.

22 Lord, You redeem my soul because I am one of Your servants. Because I take refuge in You, I am not condemned.

PP 35 PP 35

1 Lord, You contend with those who contend with me. You fight against those who fight against me.

2 You take hold of shield and buckler and You help me.

3 You brandish the spear, and You block those who pursue me. You tell my soul, "I am your salvation."

4 You disappoint those who seek after me and You bring them to dishonor. You turn back those who plot my ruin and You confound them.

5 You make them be as chaff before the wind, Your angel driving them on.

6 You cause their way to be dark and slippery, Your angel pursuing them.

7 For without cause they have hidden their net in a pit for me. Without cause they have dug a pit for me.

8 You cause destruction to come on them unawares. You cause them to be caught in their own net that they have hidden. You cause them to fall into that destruction.

9 Lord, my soul is joyful in You. It rejoices in Your salvation.

10 All my bones say, "Lord, who is like You, who delivers the poor from him who is too strong for him; yes, the poor and the needy from him who robs him?"

11 Unrighteous witnesses rise up. They ask me about things that I do not know.

12 They reward me evil for good, to the despair of my soul.

13 But as for me, when they are sick, my clothing is sackcloth. I humble my soul with fasting; I pray with my head bowed down on my chest.

14 I behave myself as though it is my friend or my brother. I bow down in mourning, as one who mourns his mother.

15 But in my adversity, they rejoice, and gather themselves together. The attackers gather themselves together against me. Adversaries that I do not know tear at me without ceasing.

16 Like profane mockers who do not acknowledge You, they gnash their teeth at me.

17 Lord, how long will You look on? But now You rescue my soul from their destruction, my precious life from the lions.

18 I give You thanks in the great assembly. I praise You among many people.

19 You do not let my enemies wrongfully rejoice over me; neither do You let those who hate me without a cause wink their eye.

20 For they do not speak peace, they devise deceitful words against me because I live quietly in the land.

21 Yes, they open their mouth wide against me. They say, "Aha! Aha! Our eye has seen it!"

22 You see it, Lord, and You do not keep silent. You are not far from me.

23 Now You wake up! You rise up to defend me, my God! My Lord, You contend for me!

24 You vindicate me, Lord my God, according to Your righteousness. You do not let them gloat over me.

25 You do not let them say in their heart, "Aha! That's the way we want it!" You do not let them say, "We have swallowed him up!"

26 You disappoint and confound all who rejoice at my calamity. You cause them to be clothed with shame and dishonor who magnify themselves against me.

27 You cause those who favor my righteous cause to shout for joy and be glad. Yes, You cause them to say continually about me, "May the Lord be magnified, who has pleasure in the prosperity of His servant!"

28 My tongue talks about your righteousness and praises You all day long.

1 A revelation is within my heart about the disobedience of the wicked: There is no fear of You, God, before Your eyes.

2 For the wicked flatters himself in his own eyes, too much to detect and hate his own sin.

3 The words of his mouth are iniquity and deceit. He ceases to be wise and to do good.

4 He plots iniquity on his bed. He sets himself in a way that is not good. He does not abhor evil.

5 But, Lord, Your loving kindness is in the heavens. Your faithfulness reaches to the skies.

6 Your righteousness is like Your mountains, God. Your judgments are like Your great deep. You preserve man and animal.

7 How precious is Your loving kindness, God! I take refuge under the shadow of Your wings.

8 I am abundantly satisfied with the abundance of Your house. You allow me to drink of the river of Your pleasures.

9 For with You is the spring of life. In Your light we see light.

10 You continue Your loving kindness to me because I know You; Your righteousness because I am upright in heart.

11 You do not let the foot of pride come against me. You do not let the hand of the wicked drive me away.

12 You make the workers of iniquity fall. You thrust them down, and they are not able to rise.

PP 37

1 I do not fret because of evildoers, neither am I envious of those who work unrighteousness.

2 For they are soon cut down like the grass, and wither like the green herb.

3 Lord, I trust in You and do good. I dwell in the land and enjoy safe pasture.

4 I delight myself in You and You give me the desires of my heart.

5 I commit my way to You; I trust in You, and You do this:

6 You make my righteousness shine like daylight, and my justice as the noon day sun.

7 I rest in You, Lord, and wait patiently for You. I do not fret because of him who prospers in his way; because of the man who makes wicked plots happen.

8 I cease from anger and forsake wrath. I do not fret; it leads only to evildoing.

9 For evildoers are cut off, but because I wait for You, Lord, I inherit the land.

10 For yet a little while, and the wicked will be no more. Yes, though I look for him, he will not be there.

11 But, because I am humble before You, I inherit the land, and delight myself in the abundance of peace.

12 The wicked plots against me because I am just, and gnashes at me with his teeth.

13 But, Lord, You laugh at him, for You see that his day is coming.

14 The wicked draw out the sword, and bend their bow, to cast me down with the poor and needy; to kill those who are upright on the path.

15 But You make their sword enter into their own heart. You break their bows.

16 Better is a little that the righteous have, than the abundance of many wicked.

17 For You, Lord, break the arms of the wicked, but You uphold me because I am righteous.

18 You know my days because I am blameless in Your sight. My inheritance is forever.

19 I am not disheartened in the times of evil. In the days of famine, I am satisfied.

20 But the wicked perish. Your enemies, Lord, are like the beauty of the fields; they vanish— vanish like smoke.

21 The wicked borrow, and do not pay back, but because I am righteous, I give generously.

22 I am blessed by You and I inherit the land. Those who are cursed by You are cut off.

23 My steps are established by You, Lord. I delight in Your way.

24 Though I stumble, I do not fall, for You hold me up with Your hand.

25 I have been young, and now am old, yet I am not forsaken because I am righteous, nor do my children beg for bread.

26 Because I am righteous, all day long I deal graciously, and lend. My offspring are blessed.

27 I depart from evil and do good. I live securely forever.

28 For You, Lord, love justice and do not forsake me. I am one of Your saints. I am preserved forever, but the children of the wicked are cut off.

29 Because I am righteous in Your sight, I inherit the land, and live in it forever.

30 Because I am righteous, my mouth speaks wisdom. My tongue speaks justice.

31 God, Your law is in my heart. None of my steps slip.

32 The wicked stalk me because I am righteous and seek to kill me.

33 But, You do not leave me in my enemy's hand, nor do You condemn me when I am judged.

34 I wait for You and keep Your way. You exalt me to inherit the land. When the wicked are cut off, I see it.

35 I have seen the wicked in great power, spreading himself like a green tree in its native soil.

36 But he passes away, and behold, he is no more. Yes, I sought him, but he could not be found.

37 You mark me because I am a blameless man in Your sight, and You see me because I am upright. There is a future for me because I am a man of peace.

38 As for transgressors, You destroy them all, together. The future of the wicked are cut off.

39 But my salvation is from You, Lord, because I am righteous. You are my stronghold in the times of trouble.

40 You, Lord, help me and rescue me. You rescue me from the wicked and save me, because I take refuge in You.

PP 38 PP 38

1 Lord, You rebuke me in Your wrath, and You chasten me in Your anger.

2 Your arrows pierce me and Your hand presses hard on me.

3 There is no soundness in my flesh because of Your indignation, neither is there any health in my bones because of my sin.

4 My iniquities have overcome me; as a heavy burden, they are too heavy for me.

5 My wounds are loathsome and corrupt because of my foolishness.

6 I am in pain and bow down low. I mourn all day long.

7 My back is filled with burning pain. There is no soundness in my flesh.

8 I am faint and severely bruised. I groan because of the anguish of my heart.

9 Lord, all my desires are before You. My groaning is not hidden from You.

10 My heart throbs. My strength fails me. The light of my eyes has also left me.

11 My lovers and my friends stand aloof from my plague. My kinsmen stand far away.

12 They who seek my life lay snares. Those who seek my hurt speak mischievous things, and plot deceitful plans all day long.

13 But I am as a deaf man and do not hear. I am as a mute man who does not open his mouth.

14 Yes, I am as a man who does not hear, in whose mouth are no answers.

15 But I hope in You and You answer me, Lord my God.

16 For I said, "Do not let them gloat over me, or exalt themselves over me when my foot slips."

17 For I am ready to fall. My pain is continually with me.

18 I declare my iniquity. I am sorry for my sin.

19 But my enemies are vigorous and strong. Those who hate me without reason are numerous.

20 They who render evil for good are also adversaries to me, because I follow what is good.

21 But You do not forsake me, Lord. My God, You are not far from me.

22 You hurry to help me, my Lord and my salvation.

1 I say, "I watch my ways, so that I do not sin with my tongue. I keep my mouth with a bridle while the wicked are before me."

2 When I was silent, I held my peace, even from speaking good. My sorrow was stirred.

3 My heart was hot within me. While I meditated, the fire burned. I spoke with my tongue:

4 "Lord, You show me my end, the measure of my days. You let me know how frail I am.

5 Behold, You make my days a hand width. My lifetime as nothing before You. Surely every man stands as a mere breath."

6 "Every man is like a shadow. He busies himself in vain. He heaps up wealth and does not know who shall receive it.

7 Lord, what do I wait for? My hope is in You.

8 You deliver me from all my transgressions. You do not make me the disdain of the foolish.

9 I remain silent. I do not open my mouth, because You do this for me.

10 You remove Your scourge from me because I am overcome by the blow of Your hand.

11 When You rebuke and correct me for iniquity, You consume my wealth like a moth. Surely every man is but a breath."

12 "You, hear my prayer, Lord, and You give ear to my cry. You are not silent at my tears. For I am a stranger with You; a foreigner, as all my fathers were.

13 You spare me, that I may recover strength, before I go away and exist no more."

PP 40 PP 40

1 I wait patiently for You, Lord. You turn to me and hear my cry.

2 You bring me up out of a horrible pit, out of the miry clay. You set my feet on a rock and give me a firm place to stand.

3 You put a new song in my mouth, even praise to You, my God. Many see it, and fear, and trust in You.

4 Blessed am I because I make You my trust, and I do not respect the proud, nor those who turn away to worthless idols.

5 Lord, my God, many are the wonderful works which You do, and Your thoughts which are towards me. They are so numerous that they cannot be declared back to You. When I declare and speak of them, they are more than can be counted.

6 Sacrifice and offerings You do not desire. You have opened my ears. You do not require burnt offerings and sin offerings.

7 Then I say, "Behold, I have come. It is written about me in the book, in the scroll.

8 I delight to do Your will, my God. Yes, Your law is within my heart."

9 I proclaim glad news of righteousness in the great assembly. Behold, I do not seal my lips, Lord; You know.

10 I do not hide Your righteousness within my heart. I declare Your faithfulness and Your salvation. I do not conceal Your loving kindness and Your truth from the great assembly.

11 You do not withhold Your tender mercies from me. Your loving kindness and Your truth continually preserve me.

12 For innumerable evils surround me. My iniquities overtake me, so that I am not able to look up. They are more than the hairs of my head. My heart fails me.

13 But You are pleased to deliver me, Lord. You hurry to help me.

14 All who seek after my soul to destroy it are disappointed and shamed. You turn them back and confuse them and bring dishonor to all who delight in my hurt.

15 You make all who tell me, "Aha! Aha!", despised because of their shame.

16 Because I seek You, I rejoice and am glad in You. Because I love Your salvation, I say continually, "Let the Lord be exalted!"

17 I am poor and needy. But You, Lord, think about me. You are my help and my deliverer, and You do not delay.

1 Blessed am I because I consider the poor and the weak. Lord, You deliver me in my day of trouble.

2 You preserve me and keep me alive. I am blessed on the earth. You do not surrender me to the will of my enemies.

3 You sustain me on my sickbed and restore me from my bed of illness.

4 I say, "Lord, You have mercy on me! You heal me, even though I have sinned against you."

5 My enemies speak evil against me: "When will he die, and his name perish?"

6 My enemy comes to see me, and he speaks falsehood. His heart gathers lies. When he goes out, he tells it to all.

7 All who hate me whisper together against me. They imagine the worst for me.

8 "An evil disease", they say, "has afflicted him. Now that he lies down, he shall rise up no more."

9 Yes, my own close friend, in whom I trust, who eats bread with me, has lifted up his heel against me.

10 But You, Lord, have mercy on me, and You raise me up, that I may repay them.

11 Because my enemy does not triumph over me, I know that You delight in me.

12 As for me, You uphold me in my integrity, and set me in Your presence forever.

13 Blessed are You, the God of Israel, from everlasting and to everlasting!
Amen and amen.

PP 42 PP 42

1 As the deer pants for water, so my soul pants for You, God.

2 My soul thirsts for You, for the living God. Soon, I will come and appear before You.

3 My tears are my food, day and night, while men continually ask me, "Where is your God?"

4 These things I remember and pour out from my soul; how I used to go with the crowd, and lead the procession to Your house, with the voice of joy and praise; a multitude keeping Your holy day.

5 Why are you in despair, my soul? Why are you disturbed within me? My hope is in You, God! I praise You for the saving help of Your presence.

6 My God, my soul is in despair within me. Therefore, I remember You from the land of the Jordan, the heights of Hermon, from the hill Mizar.

7 Deep calls to deep at the loud sound of Your waterfalls. All Your waves sweep over me.

8 Lord, You command Your loving kindness in the daytime. In the night Your song is with me; a prayer to You, God of my life.

9 I ask You, God, my Rock, "Why do You forget me? Why do I go around mourning because of the oppression of my enemy?"

10 As with a sword in my bones, my adversaries insult me, while they continually ask me, "Where is your God?"

11 Why are you in despair, my soul? Why are you disturbed within me? My hope is in You, God! I praise You, for You are the saving help of my countenance, my Savior and my God.

PP 43 PP 43

1 God, You vindicate me, and You plead my cause against an ungodly nation. You deliver me from deceitful and wicked men.

2 You are the God of my strength. Why do you reject me? Why do I go around mourning because of the oppression of my enemy?

3 Lord, You send out Your light and Your truth. They lead me. They bring me to Your holy hill, to Your tents.

4 I come to Your altar; to You, God, for You are my exceeding joy. I praise You on the harp, God, my God.

5 Why are you in despair, my soul? Why are you disturbed within me? My hope is in You, God! I praise You: my Savior, my helper, and my God.

1 God, we have heard with our ears. Our fathers have told us what works You did in their days, in the days of old.

2 You drove out the nations with Your hand, but You planted our fathers. You afflicted the peoples in those lands, and You spread our fathers abroad.

3 For they did not get possession of the land by their own sword, neither did their own arm save them; but by Your right hand, Your arm, and by the light of Your face they did these things, because You were favorable to them.

4 God, You are my King. You command victories for Jacob!

5 Through You, I push down my adversaries. Through Your name, I tread down those who rise up against me.

6 I do not trust in my bow, neither does my sword save me.

7 But You save me from my adversaries, and shame those who hate me.

8 In You, God, I make my boast all day long. I give thanks to Your name forever.

9 But now You reject me, and bring me to dishonor, and do not go out with my armies.

10 You make me turn back from my adversary. Those who hate me take plunder for themselves.

11 You have made me like sheep for food and have scattered me among the nations.

12 You sell me for nothing and have gained nothing from my sale.

13 You make me a reproach to my neighbors, a scoffing and a ridicule to those who are around me.

14 You make me a byword among the nations, a shaking of the head among the peoples.

15 All day long my dishonor is before me, and shame covers my face

16 at the taunt of those who reproach and verbally abuse me; because of my enemy who wants revenge.

17 All this has come on me, yet I do not forget You. I am not unfaithful to Your covenant.

18 My heart does not turn back, neither do my steps stray from Your path,

19 though You crush me in the haunt of jackals and cover me with the shadow of death.

20 If I have forgotten You, O God, or spread out my hands to a foreign god,

21 You search this out. For You know the secrets of my heart.

22 Yes, for Your sake I am killed all day long. I am regarded as sheep for the slaughter.

23 But You wake up! You do not sleep, Lord. You arise and You do not reject me forever!

24 You do not hide Your face or forget my affliction and my oppression.

25 For I bow down to the dust. My body clings to the earth.

26 You rise up to help me. You redeem me for Your loving kindness' sake.

PP 45

PP 45

1 Their hearts overflow with a noble theme. They recite their verses for me. Their tongues are like the pen of a skillful writer.

2 I am the most excellent of the sons of men. Grace has anointed my lips, therefore You, God, bless me forever.

3 I strap my sword on my thigh, the mighty one, in my splendor and my majesty.

4 In my majesty I ride victoriously on behalf of truth, humility, and righteousness. My right hand displays awesome deeds.

5 My arrows are sharp. The nations fall under me, with arrows in the heart of my enemies.

6 Your throne, God, is forever and ever. A scepter of uprightness is the scepter of Your kingdom.

7 I love righteousness and hate wickedness. Therefore You, God, my God, have anointed me with the oil of gladness above my associates.

8 All my garments smell like myrrh, aloes, and cassia. Out of ivory palaces, music from stringed instruments makes me glad.

9 Kings' daughters are among my honorable women. At my right hand the queen stands in gold of Ophir.

10 Listen, daughter, consider, and turn your ear. Forget your own people, and also your father's house.

11 I desire your beauty. Honor me, for I am your lord.

12 The daughter of Tyre comes with a gift. The rich among the people entreat my favor.

13 The princess is all glorious. Her clothing is interwoven with gold.

14 She is led to me in embroidered work. The virgins, her companions who follow her and are brought to her.

15 With gladness and rejoicing they are led. They enter into my palace.

16 My sons will take the place of my fathers. I make them princes in all the earth.

17 My name will be remembered in all generations. Therefore, the peoples shall give You, God, thanks forever and ever.

PP 46 PP 46

1 God, You are my refuge and strength, a very present help in trouble.

2 Therefore, I am not afraid, though the earth gives way, though the mountains are shaken into the heart of the seas;

3 though its waters roar and are turbulent, though the mountains tremble and quake.

4 There is a river, the streams of which make Your city glad, the holy place of the tents where You dwell, Lord Most High.

5 You are within her. She is not destroyed. You, God, help her at dawn.

6 Nations rage. Kingdoms are destroyed. You lift Your voice and the earth melts.

7 You, Lord, God of Armies, are with me. You, the God of Jacob, are my refuge.

8 I come and see Your works, what desolations You make on the earth.

9 You make wars cease to the ends of the earth. You break the bow and shatter the spear. You burn the chariots in the fire.

10 "Be still and know that I Am God. I am exalted among the nations. I am exalted in the earth."

11 You, Lord, God of Armies, are with me. You, the God of Jacob, are my refuge.

PP 47   PP 47

1 All the nations clap their hands. They shout to You, God, with the voice of triumph!

2 For You, God Most High, are awesome. You are the great King over all the earth.

3 You subdue nations under me, and peoples under my feet.

4 You choose my inheritance for me, the glory of Jacob whom You loved.

5 God, You have gone up with a shout; the Lord, with the sound of a trumpet.

6 I sing praises to You, God! I sing praises! I sing praises to You, my King! I sing praises!

7 For You, God, are the King of all the earth. I sing praises with understanding.

8 You reign over all the nations. You sit on Your holy throne.

9 The princes of Your peoples are gathered together; Your people, O God of Abraham. For the kings of the earth belong to You. You are greatly exalted!

PP 48   PP 48

1 Great are You, Lord, and greatly to be praised, in Your city, in Your holy mountain.

2 Beautiful in its elevation, the joy of the whole earth, is Mount Zion; on the north sides, the city of the great king, Your city.

3 You have shown Yourself in her citadels; shown Yourself as a refuge.

4 For, behold, the kings assemble themselves, and pass by together.

5 They see Your city and are amazed. They are terrified and they flee.

6 Trembling takes hold of them there; pain, as of a woman giving birth.

7 With the east wind, You break the ships of Tarshish.

8 As we hear, so we also see, in Your city, God of Armies, in Your city, O God. You establish it forever.

9 I think about Your loving kindness in the middle of Your temple.

10 As with Your name so Your praise is to the ends of the earth. Your right hand is full of righteousness.

11 Mount Zion is glad! The daughters of Judah rejoice because of Your judgments.

12 You walk about Zion and go around her. You number her towers.

13 You notice her fortifications. You consider her palaces, that You may tell it to the next generation.

14 For You are my God forever and ever. You are my guide even to death.

PP 49 PP 49

1 Hear this, all you peoples. Listen, all you inhabitants of the world,

2 both low and high, rich and poor together.

3 My mouth speaks words of wisdom. My heart utters understanding.

4 I incline my ear to a proverb. I solve my riddle on the harp.

5 I do not fear in the days of evil, when iniquity surrounds me.

6 I do not trust in my wealth, or boast in the multitude of my riches—

7 those things cannot redeem my brother, nor give You, God, a ransom for him.

8 For the redemption of his life is costly, no payment is ever enough,

9 that he should live on forever, that he should not see corruption.

10 For I see that wise men die; likewise, the fool and the senseless perish, and leave their wealth to others.

11 I do not think that my house will endure forever, nor my dwelling place to all generations. I do not name my lands after myself.

12 For man, despite his riches, does not endure. He is like the animals that perish.

13 This is the destiny of those who are foolish, and of those who approve their foolish ways.

14 They are appointed as a flock for the grave. Death devours them. As one who is upright, I have dominion over them in the morning. Their beauty decays in the grave, far from their mansion.

15 But You, God, redeem my soul from the power of the grave, for You receive me.

16 I am not impressed when a man is made rich, when the glory of his house is increased;

17 for when he dies, he will carry nothing away. His glory will not go down to the grave with him.

18 Though while he lives, he blesses his soul— and men praise him when he does well for himself—

19 he shall join the generation of his fathers. They shall never see the light.

20 A man who has riches without understanding, is like the animals that perish.

PP 50

1 You are the Mighty One, God. You speak and call the earth from sunrise to sunset.

2 Out of Zion, the perfection of beauty, You shine out.

3 You come and You do not keep silent. A fire devours before You. A raging storm is all around You.

4 You call to the heavens above, to the earth, that You may judge Your people; You say:

5 "Gather my saints together to Me, those who have made a covenant with Me by sacrifice."

6 The heavens declare Your righteousness, for You, God, are the judge.

7 You say, "Hear, My people, and I will speak. Israel, I will testify against you. I am God, your God.

8 I do not rebuke you for your sacrifices. Your burnt offerings are continually before Me.

9 I have no need for a bull from your stall, nor male goats from your pens.

10 For every animal of the forest is Mine, and the livestock on a thousand hills.

11 I know all the birds of the mountains. The wild animals of the field are Mine.

12 If I were hungry, I would not tell you, for the world is Mine, and all that is in it.

13 Will I eat the meat of bulls, or drink the blood of goats?

14 Offer to God the sacrifice of thanksgiving. Pay your vows to the Most High.

15 Call on Me in the day of trouble. I will deliver you, and you will honor Me."

16 But, Lord, to the wicked You say, "What right do you have to declare My statutes, that you have taken My covenant on your lips,

17 since you hate instruction, and throw My words behind you?

18 When you saw a thief, you consented with him, and have participated with adulterers.

19 You give your mouth to evil. Your tongue frames deceit.

20 You sit and speak against your brother. You slander your own mother's son.

21 You have done these things, and I kept silent. You thought that I was just like you. I will rebuke you and accuse you in front of your eyes.

22 Now consider this, you who forget Me, your God, lest I tear you into pieces, and there be no one to deliver you.

23 Whoever offers the sacrifice of thanksgiving glorifies Me and prepares his way so that I will show My salvation to him."

1 You have mercy on me, God, according to Your loving kindness. According to the multitude of Your tender mercies, You blot out my transgressions.

2 You wash me thoroughly from my iniquity. You cleanse me from my sin.

3 For I know my transgressions. My sin is constantly before me.

4 Against You, and You only, Lord, I have sinned, and done that which is evil in Your sight. So, You are proved right when You speak, and justified when You judge.

5 Behold, I was born in iniquity. My mother conceived me in sin.

6 Behold, You desire truth in the inward parts. You teach me wisdom in the inmost place.

7 You purify me with hyssop, and I am clean. You wash me, and I am whiter than snow.

8 You let me hear joy and gladness; even the bones which You have broken rejoice.

9 You hide Your face from my sins and blot out all of my iniquities.

10 You create in me a clean heart, O God. You renew a right spirit within me.

11 You do not throw me from Your presence, nor do You take Your Holy Spirit from me.

12 You restore to me the joy of Your salvation. You uphold me with a willing spirit.

13 I teach transgressors Your ways and sinners return to You.

14 You deliver me from the guilt of bloodshed, O God, the God of my salvation. My tongue sings aloud of Your righteousness.

15 Lord, You open my lips. My mouth declares Your praise.

16 For You do not delight in sacrifice, or else I would give it. You have no pleasure in burnt offerings.

17 The sacrifices that You desire are a broken spirit. O God, You do not despise a broken and contrite heart.

18 You make Zion do well in Your good pleasure. You build the walls of Jerusalem.

19 Then You will delight in the sacrifices of righteousness, in whole burnt offerings. Then they will offer bulls on Your altar.

PP 52 PP 52

1 God, my enemy, a mighty man, boasts of mischief. He is a disgrace before You. But Your loving kindness endures continually.

2 His tongue plots destruction, like a sharp razor, working deceitfully.

3 He loves evil more than good, lying rather than speaking the truth.

4 He loves all destructive words; he has a deceitful tongue.

5 God, You destroy my enemy forever. You harshly take him up; You pluck him out of his tent, and root him out of the land of the living.

6 The righteous also see it, and fear, and laugh at him, saying,

7 "Behold, this is the man who did not make God his strength, but trusted in the abundance of his riches, and strengthened himself in his wickedness."

8 But as for me, I am like a strong, healthy olive tree in Your house, God. I trust in Your loving kindness forever and ever.

9 In the presence of Your saints, I give You thanks forever, because You have done it. I hope in Your name, for it is good.

PP 53 PP 53

1 The fool says in his heart, "There is no God." They are corrupt and do abominable iniquities. There is no one who does good.

2 God, You look down from heaven on the children of men, to see if there are any who understand, any who seek after You.

3 Every one of them has gone away from You. They have become corrupt together. There is no one who does good, no, not one.

4 The workers of iniquity have no knowledge. They eat up Your people as men eat bread; they do not call on You, God.

5 But, You cause them to be in great fear, where there is no fear, for You scatter the bones of those who encamp against You. You put them to shame, because You reject them.

6 Oh that the salvation of Israel would come out of Zion! When You bring back Your people from captivity, then Jacob shall rejoice, and Israel shall be glad.

PP 54 PP 54

1 God, You save me by Your name; You vindicate me in Your might.

2 You hear my prayer. You listen to the words of my mouth.

3 For strangers rise up against me. Violent men seek after my soul. They do not set You before themselves.

4 Behold, God, You are my helper. You are the one who sustains my soul.

5 You repay the evil to my enemies. You destroy them in Your truth.

6 With a free will offering, I sacrifice to You. I give thanks to Your name for it is good.

7 You deliver me out of all my troubles. My eye sees triumph over my enemies.

1 God, You listen to my prayer. You do not hide Yourself from my supplication.

2 You attend to me and answer me. I am troubled in my thoughts, and moan

3 because of the voice of my enemy, because of the oppression of the wicked. For they bring suffering on me. In anger they hold a grudge against me.

4 My heart is severely pained within me. The terrors of death have fallen on me.

5 Fearfulness and trembling have come on me. Horror overwhelms me.

6 I say, "Oh that I had wings like a dove! Then I would fly away and be at rest.

7 Behold, then I would wander far off. I would lodge in the wilderness."

8 "I would hurry to a shelter from the turbulent wind and storm."

9 But, You confuse my enemies, Lord, and confound their language, because of the violence and strife that I see in the city.

10 Day and night they prowl around on its walls. Malice and abuse are also within its walls.

11 Destructive forces are within its walls. Threats and lies do not depart from its streets.

12 For it is not an enemy who insults me, then I could endure it. Neither was it he who hates me who raises himself up against me, then I would hide myself from him.

13 But it is my companion, a man like me, my close, familiar friend.

14 We took sweet fellowship together. We walked in Your house with Your people.

15 Lord, You bring death suddenly on my enemies. You send them down alive into the grave. For wickedness is among them, in their dwelling.

16 As for me, I call on You and You save me.

17 Evening, morning, and at noon, I cry out in distress to You. You hear my voice.

18 You redeem my soul in peace from the battle that is against me, although there are many who oppose me.

19 You are enthroned forever. You hear my enemies and answer them. They never change and do not fear You, God.

20 My enemy raises his hands against his friends. He violates his covenant.

21 His words are smooth as butter, but his heart is war. His words are softer than oil, yet they are drawn swords.

22 I cast my burden on You, Lord, and You sustain me. You never allow me to be moved, because I am righteous in Your sight.

23 But You, God, bring my enemies down into the pit of destruction. Bloodthirsty and deceitful men do not live out half their days, but I trust in You.

PP 56 PP 56

1 God, You are merciful to me, for men want to swallow me up. All day long, they attack and oppress me.

2 My enemies swallow me up all day long, for there are many who fight proudly against me.

3 When I am afraid, I put my trust in You.

4 God, I praise Your word. In You, God, I put my trust, and I am not afraid. Flesh can do nothing to me.

5 All day long my enemies twist my words. All their thoughts are evil against me.

6 They conspire and lurk, watching my steps. They are eager to take my life.

7 But, You do not allow them to escape by iniquity. In anger, God, You cast down my enemies.

8 You count my wanderings. You record my tears in Your scroll. They are in Your book.

9 My enemies turn back because I call to You in that day. I know this, Lord: You are for me.

10 God, I praise Your word. O Lord, I praise Your word.

11 I put my trust in You. I am not afraid. Men can do nothing to me

12 Your vows are on me, God. I give thank offerings to You.

13 For You deliver my soul from death and prevent my feet from falling. I walk before You in the light of the living.

PP 57

1 God, You are merciful to me. You are merciful to me, for my soul takes refuge in You. Yes, in the shadow of Your wings, I take refuge, until disaster has passed.

2 I cry out to You, God Most High; to You, who accomplishes Your plans for me.

3 You send from heaven and save me. You rebuke the one who is pursuing me. You send out Your loving kindness and Your truth to me.

4 My soul is among lions. I lie among those who want my destruction; the sons of men, whose teeth are spears and arrows, and their tongues are sharp swords.

5 You are exalted, God, above the heavens! Your glory is above all the earth!

6 My enemies have prepared a net for my steps. My soul is bowed down, distressed. They dig a pit before me, but they fall into the middle of it, themselves.

7 My heart is steadfast, God. My heart is steadfast. I sing praises to You.

8 My soul awakes! Also, the lute and harp wake up! I wake up the dawn.

9 I give thanks to You, Lord, among the peoples. I sing praises to You among the nations.

10 For Your great loving kindness reaches to the heavens, and Your faithfulness reaches to the skies.

11 God, You are exalted above the heavens. Your glory is over all the earth.

PP 58 PP 58

1 Do you indeed speak righteousness, you rulers? Do you judge blamelessly, you sons of men?

2 No, in your heart you plot injustice. You measure out violence with your hands on the earth.

3 You wicked go astray from the womb. You are wayward as soon as you are born, speaking lies.

4 Your poison is like the poison of a snake, like a deaf cobra that stops its ear,

5 which does not listen to the voice of charmers, no matter how skillful the charmer may be.

6 God, You break their teeth in their mouth. You break out the great teeth of the young lions.

7 You make them vanish like water that flows away. When they draw the bow, You make their arrows blunt.

8 You make them be like a snail which melts and passes away, like the stillborn child, who never sees the sun.

9 Before their pots can feel the heat of the fresh or dry thorns, You sweep away the evil ones.

10 Because I am righteous, I rejoice when I see Your vengeance. I soak my feet in the blood of the wicked.

11 Because of Your vengeance, men say, "Most certainly there is a reward for the righteous. Most certainly You are God, who judges the earth."

PP 59 PP 59

1 You deliver me from my enemies, God, my God. You set me on high from those who rise up against me.

2 You deliver me from the workers of iniquity. You save me from the bloodthirsty men.

3 You see them, God. They lie in wait for my soul. The mighty gather themselves together against me; not because I am disobedient, nor because of my sin.

4 I have done no wrong, yet they are ready to attack me, God. But You rise up and help me!

5 You, Lord God of Armies, the God of Israel, rouse Yourself to punish the nations. You show no mercy to the wicked traitors.

6 My enemies return at evening, howling like dogs, and prowl around the city.

7 You see what they spew with their mouths. Swords are in their lips. They say, "who hears us?"

8 But You, God, laugh at them. You scoff at all the nations.

9 Oh, You are my strength and I watch for You. You are my high tower.

10 You go before me with Your loving kindness. You let me see triumph over my enemies.

11 But, You do not kill them, or Your people may forget. You scatter my enemies by Your power. You bring them down. O Lord, You are my shield.

12 For the sin of their mouths, and the words of their lips, You catch them in their pride; also, for the curses and lies which they utter.

13 You consume them in Your wrath. You consume them, and they are no more. You let them know, to the ends of the earth, that You, God, rule over Jacob.

14 At evening they return. They howl like a dog and go around the city.

15 They wander up and down for food and wait all night if they are not satisfied.

16 But I sing of Your strength. Yes, I sing aloud of Your loving kindness in the morning. For you are my high tower, a refuge in the day of my distress.

17 I sing praises to You, God, for You are my strength. For You, God, are my high tower, the God of my mercy.

1 God, You have rejected me. You have broken me down. You are angry, but You restore me.

2 You make the land tremble. You tear it apart, but You mend its fractures, for it quakes.

3 You show me hard times. You make me drink wine that makes me stagger.

4 But You give me a banner because I fear you, that I may display it for Your truth.

5 You deliver me, Your beloved. You save me with Your right hand, and You answer me.

6 You speak from Your sanctuary: "I will triumph. I will divide Shechem and measure out the valley of Succoth.

7 Gilead is mine, and Manasseh is mine. Ephraim also is the defense of my head. Judah is my scepter.

8 Moab is my wash basin. I will throw my sandal on Edom. I shout in triumph over Philistia."

9 God, You bring me into the strong city. You bring me to Edom.

10 Although You reject me, and do not go out with my armies,

11 You still give me help against my enemies, for the help of man is of no value.

12 Through You, God, I achieve victory, for it is You who treads down my adversaries.

PP 61

PP 61

1 God, You hear my cry. You listen to my prayer.

2 From the end of the earth, I call to You when my heart is overwhelmed. You lead me to the rock that is higher than I.

3 For You are my refuge, a strong tower from my enemy.

4 I dwell in Your tent forever. I take refuge in the shelter of Your wings.

5 For You, God, hear my vows. You give me the heritage of those who fear Your name.

6 You prolong my life. My years are for generations.

7 I am enthroned in Your presence forever, God. You appoint Your loving kindness and truth, and they preserve me.

8 So I sing praise to Your name forever, that I may fulfill my vows daily.

PP 62

PP 62

1 God, my soul rests in You, alone. My salvation is from You.

2 You alone are my rock, my salvation, and my fortress. I am never greatly shaken.

3 How long will my enemies assault me? Will all of them throw me down, like a leaning wall or a tottering fence?

4 My enemies fully intend to throw me down from my lofty place. They delight in lies. They bless with their mouth, but they curse inwardly.

5 God, my soul waits in silence for You alone. My expectation is from You.

6 You alone are my rock and my salvation, my fortress. I am not shaken.

7 My salvation and my honor are with You, God. You are the rock of my strength, and my refuge.

8 With all Your people, I trust in You at all times. I pour out my heart before You, God. You are my refuge.

9 Surely men of low degree are just a breath, and men of high degree are a lie. In the balances they are nothing. Together, they are lighter than a breath.

10 I do not trust in oppression. I do not become proud in robbery. If riches increase, I do not set my heart on them.

11 God, You speak; twice I have heard this, that power belongs to You.

12 To You, Lord, belongs loving kindness. You reward me for my work.

PP 63 PP 63

1 God, You are my God. I earnestly seek You. My soul thirsts for You. My flesh longs for You, in a dry and weary land, where there is no water.

2 I see You in Your sanctuary. I am awed by Your power and Your glory.

3 Because Your loving kindness is better than life, my lips praise You.

4 I bless You while I live. I lift up my hands in Your name.

5 My soul is satisfied as with the richest food. My mouth praises You with joyful lips,

6 when I remember You on my bed and think about You in the night watches.

7 You are my help. I rejoice in the shadow of Your wings.

8 My soul stays close to You. Your right hand holds me up.

9 But those who seek to destroy my soul go down into the lower parts of the earth.

10 They are given over to the power of my sword. They are jackal food.

11 But I rejoice in You, God. Because I swear by You, I also praise You. Those who speak lies are silenced.

PP 64

PP 64

1 God, You hear my complaint and You preserve my life from the danger of my enemies.

2 You hide me from the conspiracy of the wicked; from the noisy crowd of those doing evil;

3 they sharpen their tongues like a sword, and aim their arrows, deadly words,

4 to shoot me from ambushes, even though I am innocent. They shoot at me suddenly and fearlessly.

5 They encourage themselves in their evil plans. They talk about laying snares secretly. They say, "Who will see them?"

6 They plot injustice, saying, "We have made a perfect plan!" Surely the mind and heart of man are cunning.

7 But God, You shoot at them. They are suddenly struck down with Your arrows.

8 Their own tongues ruin them. All who see them shake their heads.

9 All mankind is afraid. They declare Your works and wisely ponder what You do.

10 Because I am righteous in Your sight, I am glad in You and I take refuge in You. Because I am upright in heart, I praise You!

PP 65 PP 65

1 God, praise abounds to You in Zion. My vows to You are fulfilled.

2 You hear my prayer; all men come to You.

3 Sins overwhelm me, but You forgive my transgressions.

4 Blessed am I because You choose me and cause me to come near to You. I live in Your courts. I am filled with the goodness of Your house, Your holy temple.

5 By awesome deeds of righteousness, You answer me, God of my salvation. You are the hope of all the ends of the earth, of those who are far away on the sea.

6 By Your power You form the mountains, having armed Yourself with strength.

7 You still the roaring of the seas, the roaring of their waves, and the turmoil of the nations.

8 They who dwell in faraway places are afraid at Your wonders. You call the morning's dawn and the evening with songs of joy.

9 You care for the earth, and water it. You greatly enrich it. Your river, God, is full of water. You provide Your people grain, for so You have ordained it.

10 You drench the furrows of the land. You level its ridges. You soften it with showers. You bless it with a crop.

11 You crown the year with Your bounty. Your carts overflow with abundance.

12 Your wilderness grasslands overflow. Your hills are clothed with gladness.

13 Your pastures are covered with flocks. Your valleys are clothed with grain. They shout for joy! They also sing.

PP 66 PP 66

1 With all the earth, I make a joyful shout to You, God!

2 I sing to the glory of Your name! I offer glory and praise to You!

3 I say to You, "How awesome are Your deeds! Through the greatness of Your power, Your enemies submit themselves to You.

4 With all the earth, I worship You and sing to You; I sing to Your name."

5 God, I come to see what You have done on behalf of the children of men. I come to see Your awesome works.

6 You turned the sea into dry land. Your people went through the water on foot. Therefore, they rejoiced in You.

7 You rule by Your might forever. Your eyes watch the nations. You do not let the rebellious rise up against You.

8 With Your peoples, I praise You, my God! I make the sound of Your praise heard.

9 You preserve my life among the living, and do not allow my feet to slip.

10 For You test me. You refine me, as silver is refined.

11 You bring me into prison and lay a burden on my back.

12 You allow men to ride over my head. I go through fire and through water, but You bring me to Your place of abundance.

13 Then I come into Your temple with burnt offerings. I pay my vows to You,

14 which my lips promised, and my mouth spoke, when I was in distress.

15 I offer to You burnt offerings of fat animals, with the offering of rams; I offer bulls with goats.

16 God, all who fear You gather to hear. I declare what You do for my soul.

17 I cry to You with my mouth. With my tongue, I praise You.

18 If I cherished sin in my heart, You would not listen to me.

19 But most certainly, You do listen. You hear my prayer.

20 Blessed are You, God, for You do not turn away my prayer, nor withhold Your loving kindness from me.

PP 67 PP 67

1 God, You are merciful to me. You bless me and cause Your face to shine on me,

2 that Your way may be known on earth, and Your salvation among all nations.

3 I praise you with all Your peoples. All Your peoples praise You.

4 The nations are glad and sing for joy, for You judge Your peoples with righteousness, and govern the nations on earth.

5 Your peoples praise You, God. All Your peoples praise You.

6 The earth yields its increase. You, God, even my own God, bless me.

7 You bless me. All the ends of the earth fear You.

1 God, You arise and scatter Your enemies! You make all who hate You flee before You.

2 As smoke blows away, so You drive Your enemies away. As wax melts before the fire, so the wicked perish at Your presence.

3 But You make me glad because I am righteous. With all the righteous, I rejoice before You. Yes, You make me rejoice with gladness.

4 I sing to You, God! I sing praises to Your name! I extol You as You ride on the clouds. The Lord is Your name! I rejoice before You!

5 In Your holy habitation, You are a father to the fatherless, and a defender of widows.

6 You place the lonely in families. You bring out the prisoners with singing. But You make the rebellious dwell in a sun-scorched land.

7 God, when You go out before Your people, even when You march through the wilderness,

8 the earth trembles. The sky pours down rain at Your presence, the God of Sinai— at Your presence, God, the God of Israel.

9 You sent a plentiful rain. You strengthened Your inheritance when they were weary.

10 Your congregation lived in the wilderness where You provided Your goodness for the poor.

11 You announce the word. Those who proclaim it are a large company.

12 "Kings and armies flee before You! They flee! Those who wait at home divide the plunder.

13 While You sleep among the campfires, the wings of a dove were sheathed with silver, her feathers with shining gold."

14 When the You, Lord Almighty, scattered the kings in the land, it was like snow dusted on Zalmon.

15 The mountains of Bashan are majestic mountains. The mountains of Bashan are rugged.

16 Why do the rugged mountains look in envy at the mountain where You, God, choose to reign? Yes, You, Lord, dwell there forever.

17 Your chariots are tens of thousands and thousands of thousands. You are among them, Lord. You come from Sinai, into Your sanctuary.

18 When You ascend on high, You lead captives in Your train. You receive gifts among the people, yes, even from the rebellious, that You might dwell there.

19 Blessed are You, Lord, because You daily bear my burdens. You are my salvation.

20 God, You are to me the God of deliverance. You, God, the Lord, bring me escape from death.

21 But You strike through the head of Your enemies; the hairy scalp of all who continue in their wickedness.

22 You say to me, "I will bring you again from Bashan, I will bring you again from the depths of the sea,

23 that you may crush your enemies, dipping your foot in their blood, that the tongues of your dogs may have their portion from them."

24 They see Your processions, my God, my King, into Your sanctuary.

25 The singers go before the minstrels, followed by the ladies playing tambourines,

26 "Blessed are You, God, in the congregations; even You, Lord, in the assembly of Israel!"

27 There is the tribe of Benjamin, their leader, the princes of Judah, the princes of Zebulun, and the princes of Naphtali.

28 God, You command their strength. Strengthen that which You have done for us.

29 Because of Your temple at Jerusalem, kings bring gifts to You.

30 You rebuke the wild animal of the reeds, the multitude of the bulls with the calves of the peoples. You trample under foot the bars of silver. You scatter the nations who delight in war.

31 Princes come out of Egypt. Ethiopia hurries to stretch out her hands to You, God.

32 I sing to You, along with the kingdoms of the earth! I sing praises to You, Lord—

33 to You who ride on the heaven of heavens, which are of old; behold, You utter Your voice, a mighty voice.

34 I ascribe strength to You, God! Your excellency is over Israel. Your strength is in the skies.

35 You are awesome, God, in Your sanctuaries. You, the God of Israel, give strength and power to Your people. I praise You, God!

PP 69 PP 69

1 God, You save me as the waters come up to my neck!

2 I sink in deep mire, where there is no foothold. I come into deep waters, where the floods overwhelm me.

3 I am weary with my crying. My throat is dry. My eyes fail looking for You, my God.

4 Those who hate me without a cause are more than the hairs of my head. Those who want to cut me off, my wrongful enemies, are mighty. They require me to restore what I did not take away.

5 God, You know my foolishness. My sins are not hidden from You.

6 You do not let those who hope in You be shamed because of me, Lord, God of Armies. You do not let those who seek You be brought to dishonor because of me, God of Israel.

7 For your sake, God, I endure reproach. Shame covers my face.

8 I am a stranger to my brothers, an alien to my mother's children.

9 For the zeal of Your house consumes me. The accusations of those who accuse You fall on me.

10 When I weep and I fast, I endure insults.

11 When I make sackcloth my clothing, I become a byword to them.

12 Those who sit in the gates ridicule me. I am the song of the drunkards.

13 But my prayer is to You, God, at Your acceptable time. In the abundance of Your loving kindness, You answer me in the truth of Your salvation.

14 You deliver me out of the mire, and You do not let me sink. You deliver me from those who hate me, and out of the deep waters.

15 You do not let the flood waters overwhelm me, neither do You let the deep swallow me up. You do not let the pit shut its mouth on me.

16 You answer me, God, for Your loving kindness is good. According to the multitude of Your tender mercies, You turn to me.

17 You do not hide Your face from me, Your servant, for I am in distress. You answer me swiftly!

18 You draw near to my soul and redeem it. You ransom me because of my enemies.

19 You know my reproach, my shame, and my dishonor. My adversaries are all before You.

20 Insults have broken my heart, and I am full of heaviness. I look for someone to take pity, but there is no one; for comforters, but I find none.

21 They give me poison for my food. In my thirst, they give me vinegar to drink.

22 But You, Lord, make their table before them become a snare. You make it become a retribution and a trap.

23 You darken their eyes so that they cannot see. You make their backs be continually bent.

24 You pour out Your anger on them. The fierceness of Your anger overtakes them.

25 You make their habitation be desolate. You let no one dwell in their tents.

26 For they persecute me, the one You have wounded. They tell of the sorrow of those whom You hurt.

27 But You charge them with crime upon crime. You do not let them come into Your righteousness.

28 You blot them out of Your book of life, so that they are not written with the righteous.

29 I am in pain and distress, but Your salvation, God, protects me.

30 I praise Your name with a song and magnify You with thanksgiving.

31 It pleases You, Lord God, more than an ox, or a bull that has horns and hoofs.

32 Because I am humble before You, I see it, and I am glad. Because I seek after You, my heart lives.

33 For You, Lord God, hear me. You do not despise Your captive people, of whom I am one.

34 Heaven and earth praise You, along with the seas, and everything that moves therein!

35 For You save me, with Your people of Zion, and You rebuild the cities of Judah. Your people settle there and own it.

36 My children inherit the land because I am one of Your servants. Because I love Your name, I dwell there.

PP 70   PP 70

1 God, You hurry to deliver me. You come quickly to help me.

2 You disappoint and confound those who seek my soul. You turn back in disgrace those who desire my ruin.

3 In their shame, You turn back those who say to me, "Aha! Aha!"

4 Because I seek You, I rejoice, and I am glad in You. With all those who love Your salvation, I continually say, "Let God be exalted!"

5 But, God, I am poor and needy, so You come to me quickly. You are my help and my deliverer. You do not delay.

 PP 71

1 God, in You I take refuge. I am never shamed because of You.

2 You deliver me in Your righteousness, and You rescue me. You turn Your ear to me and save me.

3 You are my rock of refuge to which I always turn. You give the command to save me, for You are my rock and my fortress.

4 You rescue me, my God, from the hand of the wicked, from the hand of the unrighteous and cruel man.

5 You are my hope, Lord God; my confidence from the time of my youth.

6 I have relied on You from the womb. You took me out of my mother's womb. I always praise You.

7 I am a marvel to many, but You are my strong refuge.

8 My mouth is filled with Your praise; with Your honor all day long.

9 You do not reject me in my old age. You do not forsake me when my strength fails.

10 For my enemies talk about me. Those who want to take my life conspire together,

11 saying, "God has forsaken him. Pursue and take him, for no one will rescue him."

12 But, You are not far from me. You hurry to help me.

13 You disappoint and consume my accusers. You cover those who want to harm me with disgrace and scorn.

14 But I always hope in You and will always praise You more.

15 My mouth tells about Your righteousness, and of Your salvation all day, though I do not know its full measure.

16 I declare Your mighty acts, Lord God. I declare Your righteousness, Yours and Yours alone.

17 God, You have taught me from my youth. I declare Your wondrous works.

18 Yes, even when I am old and gray haired, You will not forsake me. I declare Your strength to the next generation, Your might to everyone who is to come.

19 Your righteousness reaches to the heavens. You do great things. No one is like You.

20 You have shown me many and bitter troubles, but You let me live. You bring me up again from the depths of the earth.

21 You increase my honor and comfort me again.

22 I praise You with the harp for Your faithfulness, my God. I sing praises to You with the lyre, Holy One of Israel.

23 My lips shout for joy! My soul, which You have redeemed, sings praises to You!

24 My tongue declares Your righteousness all day long. My enemies, who want to harm me, are shamed and confused by You.

1 God, You give me Your justice; Your righteousness to me, Your son.

2 You judge Your people with righteousness, and the poor with justice.

3 Your mountains bring prosperity to the people. Your hills bring the fruit of righteousness.

4 You judge the poor of the people. You save the children of the needy and break the oppressor in pieces.

5 They fear You as long as the sun and the moon endure, throughout all generations.

6 You come down like rain on the mown grass, as showers that water the earth.

7 In Your days, the righteous flourish, and there is an abundance of peace, until the moon is no more.

8 You have dominion from sea to sea, from the river to the ends of the earth.

9 Those who dwell in the wilderness bow before You. Your enemies lick the dust.

10 The kings of Tarshish and of the distant lands bring tribute to You. The kings of Sheba and Seba offer gifts.

11 Yes, all kings bow down before You. All nations serve You.

12 You deliver me when I cry to You, because I am poor and needy with no helper.

13 You have pity on me with the poor and needy. You save the souls of all the needy.

14 You redeem my soul from oppression and violence. My blood is precious in Your sight.

15 Lord, You live; and Sheba's gold is given to You. Men pray to You continually. They bless You all day long.

16 You make an abundance of grain throughout the land. Its fruit flourishes like Lebanon, thriving like the grass of the field.

17 Your name endures forever. Your name continues as long as the sun. Men are blessed by You. All nations call You blessed.

18 Praise be to You, Lord God, the God of Israel; You alone do marvelous deeds.

19 Blessed is Your glorious name forever! The whole earth is filled with Your glory! Amen and amen.

20 These are the prayers of Your servant.

PP 73 PP 73

1 God, You are good to Israel and to those who are pure in heart.

2 But as for me, my feet were almost gone. My steps had nearly slipped.

3 For I was envious of the arrogant, when I saw the prosperity of the wicked.

4 For they have no struggles throughout their life, and their strength is firm.

5 They are free from burdens of men. Neither are they plagued like other men.

6 Therefore pride is like a chain around their neck. Violence covers them like a garment.

7 Their eyes bulge with fat. Their minds pass the limits of conceit.

8 They ridicule and speak with malice. In arrogance, they threaten oppression.

9 They set their claim to the heavens. Their tongues claim the earth.

10 Therefore their people return to them, and they drink up waters of abundance.

11 They say, "How does God know? Will the Most High have knowledge of what we do?"

12 Behold, these are the wicked. Being always at ease, they increase in riches.

13 It seems that I cleanse my heart in vain, and wash my hands in innocence,

14 for all day long I am plagued and punished every morning.

15 If I had said, "I will speak thus", behold, I would have betrayed the generation of your children.

16 When I try to understand this, it is too painful for me—

17 but I enter Your sanctuary, God, and consider the end of the wicked.

18 Surely You set them in slippery places. You throw them down to destruction.

19 How they are suddenly destroyed! They are completely swept away with terrors.

20 As with a dream when one wakes up, so You despise their fantasies when You awake, Lord.

21 For my soul is grieved. I am embittered in my heart.

22 I am so senseless and ignorant. I am as a brute beast before you.

23 Nevertheless, I am continually with You. You hold my right hand.

24 You guide me with Your counsel, then You receive me to Your glory.

25 Lord, I have You in heaven! There is no one on earth whom I desire besides You.

26 My flesh and my heart fail, but You are the strength of my heart and my portion forever.

27 Those who are far from You perish. You destroy all those who are unfaithful to You.

28 But it is good for me to come close to You, God. I make You my refuge, that I may tell of all Your works.

1 God, why have You rejected me? Why does Your anger burn against me, one of the sheep of Your pasture?

2 Still, You remember Your congregation, which You purchased of old, which You redeemed to be the tribe of Your inheritance: Mount Zion, in which You live.

3 You turn Your feet to the perpetual ruins, all the evil that the enemy has done in Your sanctuary.

4 Your enemies roared in the middle of Your assembly. They set up their standards as signs.

5 They behaved like men wielding axes cutting through a thicket of trees.

6 Now they break all the carved work with axes and hammers.

7 They burned Your sanctuary to the ground. They profaned the dwelling place of Your name.

8 They said in their heart, "We will crush them completely." They burned up all the places in the land where You were worshiped.

9 We see no miraculous signs. There is no longer any prophet, neither is there among us anyone who knows how long this will last.

10 God, how long shall the adversary insult You? Shall the enemy blaspheme Your name forever?

11 Why do You draw back Your hand, even Your right hand? Take out Your right hand and consume them!

12 Yet You are my King of old working salvation throughout the earth.

13 You divide the sea by Your strength. You break the heads of the sea monsters in the waters.

14 You break the heads of Leviathan in pieces. You give him as food to the people and the desert creatures.

15 You open up springs and streams. You dry up mighty rivers.

16 The day is Yours; the night is also Yours. You prepare the light and the sun.

17 You set all the boundaries of the earth. You make the summer and the winter.

18 Lord, You remember that the enemy has mocked You. Foolish people have blasphemed Your name.

19 You do not deliver my soul, the soul of Your dove, to wild beasts. I am poor, but You never forget my life.

20 You honor Your covenant, for haunts of violence fill the dark places of the earth.

21 I am oppressed, but You do not let me return ashamed. With all the poor and needy, I praise Your name.

22 God, You arise and plead Your own cause! You remember how the foolish man mocks You all day.

23 You do not forget the voice of Your enemies. The turmoil of those who rise up against You ascends continually.

1 God, I give You thanks. I give thanks, for Your name is near. I tell about Your wondrous works.

2 Lord, You say, "I choose the appointed time and I judge blamelessly.

3 The earth and all its inhabitants quake, but I firmly hold its pillars.

4 I say to the arrogant, 'Do not boast!' I say to the wicked, 'Do not lift up your horn.

5 Do not lift up your horn to heaven. Do not speak with a stiff neck.'"

6 For neither from the east, nor from the west, nor yet from the south, comes exaltation of man.

7 But You, God, are the judge. You put down one and lift up another.

8 For in Your hand there is a cup, full of foaming wine mixed with spices. You pour it out and the wicked of the earth drink it to its very dregs.

9 But I will declare this forever: I sing praises to You, the God of Jacob.

10 You cut off all the horns of the wicked, but the horns of the righteous, You lift up.

1 God, in Judah You are known. Your name is great in Israel.

2 Your tabernacle is also in Salem. Your dwelling place in Zion.

3 There You broke the flaming arrows of the bow, the shield, and the sword, and the weapons of war.

4 You are glorious and excellent; more splendid than mountains filled with game.

5 Valiant men lie plundered, they sleep their last sleep. None of the men of war can lift their hands.

6 At Your rebuke, God of Jacob, both chariot and horse are cast into a dead sleep.

7 Only You are to be feared. No one can stand in Your sight when You are angry.

8 You pronounce judgment from heaven. The earth fears and is silent.

9 When You arise to judge, You save all the afflicted ones of the earth.

10 Your wrath against wicked men brings You praise. The survivors of Your wrath are restrained.

11 I make vows to You, God, and fulfill them! All the nations bring presents to You because they fear You.

12 You cut off the spirit of princes. You are feared by the kings of the earth.

1 God, my cry goes up to You! Indeed, I cry to You for help, and You listen to me.

2 In the day of my trouble I seek You. My hand is stretched out in the night and does not get tired. My soul refuses to be comforted.

3 I remember You, and I groan. I complain and my spirit is overwhelmed.

4 You hold my eyelids open. I am so troubled that I cannot speak.

5 I consider the days of old; the years of ancient times.

6 I remember my song in the night. I consider in my own heart; my spirit diligently inquires:

7 "Lord, will You reject me forever? Are You no longer favorable to me?

8 Has Your loving kindness vanished forever? Does Your promise fail for generations?

9 Have You forgotten Your mercy to me? Have You, in anger, withheld Your compassion?"

10 But then I say, "I appeal to the years of Your right hand, Lord Most High."

11 I remember Your deeds and remember Your wonders of old.

12 I meditate on all Your work and consider Your strong deeds.

13 God, Your way is in the sanctuary. There is no god as great as You.

14 You are the God who does wonders. You make Your strength known among the peoples.

15 With Your strong arm, You redeem me with all Your people, the sons of Jacob and Joseph.

16 The waters see You, God. The waters see You, and they writhe. The depths also convulse.

17 The clouds pour out water. The skies resound with thunder. Your arrows flash around.

18 The voice of Your thunder is in the whirlwind. The lightnings light up the world. The earth trembles and shakes.

19 You lead me through the sea; Your paths are through the great waters, but Your footsteps are hidden.

20 You lead Your people like a flock, by the hand of Moses and Aaron.

PP 78   PP 78

1 Lord I hear Your teaching, along with all Your people. I turn my ears to the words of Your mouth.

2 You open Your mouth in parables. You utter hidden sayings of old,

3 which I have heard and known, and my fathers have told me.

4 I do not hide these things from my children. I tell to the generation to come of Your praises, Your strength, and Your wondrous deeds that You have done.

5 For You established a covenant for Jacob, and appointed a teaching in Israel, which You commanded my fathers, that they should make them known to their children,

6 that the generation to come might know, even the children who should be born, who should arise and tell their children,

7 that they might set their hope in You, God, and not forget Your deeds, but keep Your commandments,

8 and might not act as their fathers— a stubborn and rebellious generation, a generation that did not make their hearts loyal to You. Their spirit was not steadfast with You.

9 The children of Ephraim, being armed and carrying bows, turned back in the day of battle.

10 They did not keep Your covenant and refused to walk in Your law.

11 They forgot Your doings, Your wondrous deeds that You showed to them.

12 You did marvelous things in the sight of their fathers, in the land of Egypt, in the field of Zoan.

13 You split the sea and caused them to pass through. You made the waters stand as a heap.

14 In the daytime You also led them with a cloud, and all night with the light of a pillar of fire.

15 You split rocks in the wilderness and gave them drink abundantly as out of the depths.

16 You brought streams also out of the rock and caused waters to run down like rivers.

17 Yet they still went on to sin against You, to rebel against You, the Most High, in the desert.

18 They tested You in their heart by asking for food that they desired.

19 Yes, they spoke against You, God. They said, "Can God prepare a table in the wilderness?

20 Behold, He struck the rock, so that waters gushed out, and streams overflowed. Can He give bread also? Will He provide meat for His people?"

21 Therefore You heard and were angry. A fire was kindled against Jacob, anger also went up against Israel,

22 because they did not believe in You and did not trust in Your salvation.

23 Yet You commanded the skies above and opened the doors of heaven.

24 You rained down manna on them to eat and gave them food from the sky.

25 Man ate the bread of angels. You sent them food to the full.

26 You caused the east wind to blow in the sky. By Your power You guided the south wind.

27 You also rained meat on them as thick as the dust; winged birds as numerous as the sand of the seas.

28 You let the birds fall in the middle of their camp; around their tents.

29 So they ate and were well filled. You gave them their own desire.

30 But, they did not turn from their cravings. Their food was still in their mouths,

31 when Your anger, God, went up against them. You killed some of their strongest and struck down the young men of Israel.

32 After all this they still sinned and did not believe in Your wondrous works.

33 Therefore You consumed their days in uselessness, and their years in terror.

34 Whenever You killed them, then they inquired after You. They returned and sought You earnestly.

35 They remembered that You were their rock; the Most High God, their redeemer.

36 But they flattered You with their mouth and lied to You with their tongue.

37 For their heart was not right with You, neither were they faithful in Your covenant.

38 But You, being merciful, forgave their iniquity, and did not destroy them. Yes, many times You turned Your anger away, and did not stir up all Your wrath.

39 You remembered that they were but flesh, a wind that passes away, and does not come again.

40 How often they rebelled against You in the wilderness and grieved You in the desert!

41 They turned again and tested You, and provoked You, the Holy One of Israel.

42 They did not remember Your hand, nor the day when You redeemed them from their adversary;

43 how You displayed Your signs in Egypt, Your wonders in the field of Zoan.

44 You turned their rivers into blood, and their streams, so that they could not drink.

45 You sent among them swarms of flies, which devoured them; and frogs, which destroyed them.

46 You also gave their fields to the caterpillar, and their fruit to the locust.

47 You destroyed their vines with hail, their sycamore fig trees with frost.

48 You also gave over their livestock to the hail, and their flocks to hot thunderbolts.

49 You threw on them the fierceness of Your anger, wrath, indignation, and trouble; a band of devastating angels.

50 You made a path for Your anger. You did not spare their soul from death, but gave their life over to the plague,

51 and struck down all the firstborn in Egypt, the chief of their strength in the tents of Ham.

52 But You led out Your own people like sheep and guided them in the wilderness like a flock.

53 You led them safely, so that they were not afraid, but the sea overwhelmed their enemies.

54 You brought them to the border of Your sanctuary, to Your mountain, which Your right hand had taken.

55 You also drove out the nations before them, allotted land as an inheritance for them by tribe, and made the tribes of Israel to dwell in their tents.

56 Yet they tested and rebelled against You, the Most High God, and did not keep Your commands.

57 Instead they turned back and dealt treacherously like their fathers. They were twisted like a deceitful bow.

58 For they provoked You to anger with their high places and moved You to jealousy with their engraved images.

59 When You heard this, You were angry, and greatly abhorred Israel,

60 so that You abandoned the tent of Shiloh, the tent which You placed among men,

61 and delivered Your people, Your strength, into captivity; Your glory into the adversary's hand.

62 You also gave Your people over to the sword and were angry with Your inheritance.

63 Fire devoured their young men. Their virgins had no wedding song.

64 Their priests fell by the sword, and their widows could not weep.

65 Then You, Lord, awakened as one out of sleep; like a mighty man who shouts by reason of wine.

66 You struck Your adversaries and turned them back. You put them in perpetual shame.

67 Moreover You rejected the tent of Joseph, and did not choose the tribe of Ephraim,

68 but You chose the tribe of Judah; Mount Zion which You loved.

69 You built Your sanctuary like the heights, like the earth which You have established forever.

70 You also chose David Your servant and took him from the sheepfolds,

71 from following the ewes that have their young, You brought him to be the shepherd of Jacob, Your people, and Israel, Your inheritance.

72 So David was their shepherd according to the integrity of his heart and guided them by the skillfulness of his hands.

1 God, the nations have come into Your inheritance, the land of Your people. They have defiled Your holy temple. They have destroyed Jerusalem and laid it in heaps.

2 They have given the dead bodies of Your servants to be food for the birds of the sky; the flesh of Your saints to the animals of the earth.

3 They have shed their blood like water around Jerusalem. There was no one to bury them.

4 We have become an object of reproach to our neighbors; an object of scoffing and ridicule to those who are around us.

5 How long, Lord? Will You be angry forever? Will Your jealousy burn like fire?

6 But still, You pour out Your wrath on the nations that do not know You, on the kingdoms that do not call on Your name,

7 for they have devoured Jacob and destroyed his homeland.

8 Lord, because I am counted among Your people, You do not hold the iniquities of my forefathers against me. You cause Your tender mercies to quickly meet me, for I am in desperate need.

9 You help me, God of my salvation, for the glory of Your name. You deliver me, and forgive my sins, for Your name's sake.

10 Why should the nations say, "Where is his God?" You make it be known among the nations, before our eyes, that vengeance for Your servants' blood is being poured out.

11 You hear my sighing because I am a prisoner; my sighs come before You. According to the greatness of Your power, You preserve me, even though I am sentenced to death.

12 You pay back to my neighbors seven times into their hands their sins with which they have sinned against You, Lord.

13 So we, Your people and sheep of Your pasture, give You thanks forever. We praise You forever, to all generations.

PP 80 PP 80

1 You hear me, Shepherd of Israel. You lead Joseph like a flock. You sit above the cherubim and shine out.

2 Before Ephraim and Benjamin and Manasseh, You stir up Your might! You come to save us!

3 You also restore me, God. You cause Your face to shine, and I am saved along with all of Your people.

4 Lord, God of Armies, how long will You be angry against my prayer and the prayer of Your people?

5 You have fed me with the bread of tears and given me tears to drink in large measure.

6 You make me a source of contention to my neighbors. My enemies ridicule me.

7 But still, You restore me again, God of Armies. You cause Your face to shine, and I am saved.

8 You brought a vine out of Egypt; Your people, Israel. You drove out the nations and planted it.

9 You cleared the ground for it. It took deep root, filling the land.

10 The mountains were covered with its shadow. Its boughs were like Your cedars.

11 It sent out its branches to the sea, its shoots to the river.

12 But now, Lord, why have You broken down its walls, so that all those who pass by pluck its grapes?

13 The boar out of the wood ravages it. The wild animals of the field feed on it.

14 But still, You return to Your vine, God of Armies. You look down from heaven, and see, and protect Your vine;

15 the stock which Your right hand planted; the branch that You made strong for Yourself.

16 You do not let it be burned with fire. You do not cut it down. Your people do not perish at Your rebuke.

17 Your hand is on the man of Your right hand; on the son of man whom You made strong for Yourself.

18 So we do not turn away from You. You revive us, and we call on Your name.

19 You return to us again, Lord, God of Armies. You cause Your face to shine, and we are saved.

1 I sing aloud to You, God, my strength! I make a joyful shout to You, God of Jacob!

2 I raise to You a song and bring the tambourine; the pleasant lyre with the harp.

3 I blow the trumpet at the new moon, at the full moon, on our feast day.

4 For it is a statute for Israel, an ordinance from You, God of Jacob.

5 You appointed it for Joseph as a covenant, when he went to the land of Egypt. He heard a language that he did not know.

6 You said to Your people, "I removed your shoulder from the burden. I freed your hands from the basket.

7 You called to Me in your trouble, and I delivered you. I answered you in the secret place of thunder. I tested you at the waters of Meribah."

8 "Hear, My people, and I will testify to you, Israel, if you would listen to Me!

9 There shall be no strange god in you, neither shall you worship any foreign god.

10 I am the Lord, your God, who brought you up out of the land of Egypt. Open your mouth wide, and I will fill it.

11 But My people did not listen to My voice. Israel desired none of Me.

12 So I let them go after the stubbornness of their hearts, that they might walk in their own counsels.

13 Oh that My people would listen to Me, that Israel would walk in My ways!

14 I would quickly subdue their enemies and turn My hand against their adversaries.

15 Those who hate Me would cringe before Me, and their punishment would last forever.

16 But I would have also fed them with the finest of the wheat. I will satisfy you with honey out of the rock."

PP 82 PP 82

1 God, You preside in the great assembly. You judge among the "gods".

2 You say, "How long will you judge unjustly, and show partiality to the wicked?"

3 "You are to defend the weak, the poor, and the fatherless. You must maintain the rights of the poor and the oppressed.

4 You must rescue the weak and needy and deliver them out of the hand of the wicked.

5 They do not know anything, neither do they understand. They walk back and forth in darkness. All the foundations of the earth are shaken.

6 I said, 'You are gods; all of you are sons of the Most High'.

7 Nevertheless you shall die like men and fall like all of the rulers."

8 Then You arise, God, and judge the earth, for all of the nations are Yours.

──────◇──────

1 God, You do not keep silent. You do not keep silent, and You are not still.

2 For, behold, Your enemies are stirred up. Those who hate You lift up their heads.

3 They conspire with cunning against me and Your people. They plot against Your cherished ones, of whom I am one.

4 "Come," they say, "let us destroy them as a nation, that the name of Israel may be remembered no more."

5 For they conspire together with one mind. They form an alliance against You.

6 The tents of Edom and the Ishmaelites, Moab, and the Hagrites,

7 Gebal, Ammon, and Amalek and Philistia with the inhabitants of Tyre.

8 Assyria also is joined with them. They have helped the children of Lot.

9 You do to them as You did to Midian, as to Sisera, as to Jabin, at the river Kishon,

10 who perished at Endor, who became as dung for the earth.

11 You make their nobles like Oreb and Zeeb, yes, all their princes like Zebah and Zalmunna,

12 who said, "Let's take possession of God's pasture lands."

13 You, my God, make them like tumbleweed; like chaff before the wind.

14 As the fire that burns the forest, as the flame that sets the mountains on fire,

15 so You pursue them with Your tempest and terrify them with Your storm.

16 You fill their faces with shame, and they seek Your name.

17 You shame and discourage them forever. Yes, You confuse them and make them perish,

18 that they may know that You alone, Lord God Almighty, are the Most High over all the earth.

PP 84 PP 84

1 How lovely are Your dwellings, Lord, God of Armies!

2 My soul longs, and even faints for Your courts. My heart and my flesh cry out for You, the living God.

3 Yes, the sparrow has found a home, and the swallow a nest for herself, where she may have her young, near Your altars, Lord, God of Armies, my King, and my God.

4 Blessed am I and all those who dwell in Your house. I am always praising You.

5 Blessed am I and those whose strength is in You. I have set my heart on a pilgrimage.

6 Passing through the Valley of Weeping, I make it a place of springs. Yes, the autumn rain covers it with blessings.

7 I go from strength to strength. With every one of Your people, I appear before You, God, in Zion.

8 Lord, God of Armies, You hear my prayer. You listen, God of Jacob.

9 Lord, God my shield, You look at my face, as one of Your anointed.

10 For one day in Your courts is better than a thousand anywhere else. I would rather be a doorkeeper in Your house than to dwell in the tents of wickedness.

11 For You, God, are a sun and a shield. You give grace and glory. You withhold no good thing from me, because I walk blamelessly before You.

12 Lord, God of Armies, I am blessed because I trust in You.

PP 85

PP 85

1 God, You are favorable to Your land. You restore the fortunes of Jacob.

2 You forgive my iniquity and that of Your people. You cover all my sins.

3 You take away all Your wrath. You turn from the fierceness of Your anger.

4 You restore me, God of my salvation, and cause Your indignation towards me to cease.

5 You will not be angry with me forever. You will not be angry for all generations.

6 You revive me again, that I may rejoice in You.

7 Lord God, You show me Your loving kindness, and grant me Your salvation.

8 I hear what You speak, for You speak peace to Your people, Your saints, and You do not let them turn again to folly.

9 Your salvation is near to me and all those who fear You, that Your glory may dwell in our land.

10 Mercy and truth meet together. Righteousness and peace kiss each other.

11 Truth springs out of the earth. Righteousness looks down from heaven.

12 Yes, You, Lord, give that which is good. My land yields its increase.

13 Righteousness goes before You and prepares the way for Your steps.

PP 86 PP 86

1 Lord, You hear me and answer me, for I am poor and needy.

2 You preserve my soul, for I am godly. You save me, Your servant, because I trust in You.

3 You are merciful to me for I call to You all day long.

4 You bring joy to my soul. I am Your servant, Lord, and I lift up my soul to You.

5 For You are good, and ready to forgive. You are abundant in loving kindness to me and to all those who call on You.

6 You hear my prayer. You listen to the voice of my petitions.

7 In my day of trouble I call on You, and You answer me.

8 There is no one like You among the gods, Lord, nor any deeds like Your deeds.

9 You make all nations come and worship before You. They glorify Your name.

10 For You are great and do wondrous things. You are God alone.

11 You teach me Your ways. I walk in Your truth. You make my heart steadfast so that I fear Your name.

12 I praise You, Lord my God, with my whole heart. I glorify Your name forever more.

13 Your loving kindness is great towards me. You deliver my soul from the lowest grave.

14 God, the proud rise up against me. A company of violent men seek after my soul, and they do not respect You.

15 But You are a merciful and gracious God, slow to anger, and abundant in loving kindness and truth.

16 You turn to me and have mercy on me! You give me Your strength. You save my son because I am Your faithful servant.

17 God, You show me a sign of Your goodness, so that those who hate me may see it, and be shamed, because You help me and comfort me.

PP 87 PP 87

1 Lord, Your foundation is in the holy mountains.

2 You love the gates of Zion more than all the dwellings of Jacob.

3 I speak glorious things about you, city of God.

4 You say, "I record Rahab and Babylon among those who acknowledge Me. Behold, Philistia, Tyre, and also Ethiopia."

5 Yes, of Zion it is said, "This one and that one was born in her;" You, Lord Most High, establish her.

6 When You record the peoples, You say, "This one was born in the city of God."

7 All those who sing and dance say, "All my springs are in You."

PP 88 PP 88

1 Lord, God of my salvation, I cry day and night before You.

2 My prayer enters into Your presence. You turn Your ear to my cry.

3 For my soul is full of troubles. My life draws near to the grave.

4 I am counted among those who go down into the pit. I am like a man who has no help,

5 set apart among the dead, like the slain who lie in the grave, whom You remember no more. I am cut off from Your hand.

6 You have laid me in the lowest pit, in the darkest depths.

7 Your wrath lies heavily on me. You have afflicted me with all Your waves.

8 You have taken my friends from me. You have made me an abomination to them. I am confined, and I cannot escape.

9 My eyes are dim from grief. I call on You daily, Lord. I spread out my hands to You.

10 You do not show wonders to the dead. Departed spirits do not rise up and praise You.

11 Your loving kindness is not declared in the grave; nor Your faithfulness in destruction.

12 Your wonders are not made known in the dark; nor Your righteousness in the land of the forgotten.

13 But to You, Lord, I cry. In the morning, my prayer comes before You.

14 You do not reject my soul. You do not hide Your face from me.

15 I am afflicted and ready to die since the days of my youth. While I suffer Your terrors, I am hopeless.

16 Your fierce wrath goes over me. Your terrors cut me off.

17 They come around me like water all day long. They completely engulf me.

18 You have put my loved ones and close friends far from me. Darkness is now my closest friend.

PP 89 PP 89

1 Lord, I sing of Your loving kindness forever. With my mouth, I make known Your faithfulness to all generations.

2 I indeed declare, "Your love stands firm forever. You established the heavens. Your faithfulness is in them."

3 You said, "I have made a covenant with My chosen one, I have sworn to David, My servant,

4 'I will establish your offspring forever and build up your throne for all generations.'"

5 The heavens praise Your wonders, Lord. Your faithfulness also in the assembly of the holy ones.

6 For no one in the skies can be compared to You, Lord. No one among the sons of the heavenly beings is like You.

7 You are a very awesome God in the council of the holy ones. You are feared above all those who are around You.

8 Lord, God of Armies, no one is mighty like You. Your faithfulness is all around You.

9 You rule the raging sea. When its waves rise up, You calm them.

10 You break Rahab in pieces, like one of the slain. You scatter Your enemies with Your mighty arm.

11 The heavens are Yours. The earth also is Yours, the world and its fullness. You founded them.

12 You created the north and the south. Tabor and Hermon rejoice in Your name.

13 You have a mighty arm. Your hand is strong, and Your right hand is exalted.

14 Righteousness and justice are the foundation of Your throne. Loving kindness and truth go before Your face.

15 Blessed am I with all the people who learn to praise You. I walk in the light of Your presence, Lord.

16 In Your name I rejoice all day. In Your righteousness, I am exalted.

17 For You are the glory of my strength. In Your favor, my horn is exalted.

18 For my shield belongs to You, my King, the Holy One of Israel.

19 In the past, You spoke in a vision to Your saints, and said, "I have given strength to the warrior. I have exalted a young man from the people.

20 I have found David, My servant. I have anointed him with My holy oil,

21 with whom My hand shall be established. My arm will also strengthen him.

22 No enemy will tax him. No wicked man will oppress him.

23 I will beat down his adversaries before him, and strike those who hate him.

24 But My faithfulness and My loving kindness will be with him. In My name, his horn will be exalted.

25 I will set his hand also on the sea, and his right hand on the rivers.

26 He will call to Me, 'You are my Father, my God, and the rock of my salvation!'

27 I will also appoint him My firstborn, the highest of the kings of the earth.

28 I will keep My loving kindness for him forever more. My covenant will stand firm with him.

29 I will also make his offspring endure forever, and his throne as the days of heaven.

30 If his children forsake My law, and do not walk in My ordinances;

31 if they break My statutes, and don't keep My commandments;

32 then I will punish their sin with the rod, and their iniquity with stripes.

33 But I will not completely take My loving kindness from him, nor allow my faithfulness to fail.

34 I will not break My covenant, nor alter what My lips have uttered.

35 Once I have sworn by My holiness, I will not lie to David.

36 His offspring will endure forever, his throne like the sun before Me.

37 It will be established forever like the moon, the faithful witness in the sky."

38 But You have rejected and spurned and are angry with Your anointed.

39 You have renounced the covenant of Your servant. You have defiled his crown in the dust.

40 You have broken down all his hedges. You have brought his strongholds to ruin.

41 All who pass by the way rob him. He has become a reproach to his neighbors.

42 You have exalted the right hand of his adversaries. You have made all of his enemies rejoice.

43 Yes, You turn back the edge of his sword, and have not supported him in battle.

44 You have ended his splendor and thrown his throne down to the ground.

45 You have shortened the days of his youth. You have covered him with shame.

46 How long, Lord? Will You hide Yourself forever? How long will Your wrath burn like fire?

47 Remember how short my time is. For what uselessness You have created all the children of men!

48 What man shall live and not see death? Who shall deliver his soul from the power of the grave?

49 Lord, where is Your former loving kindness, which You swore to David in Your faithfulness?

50 Remember, Lord, the insults I have endured because I am Your servant; how I bear in my heart the taunts of all the mighty peoples;

51 the insults with which Your enemies have mocked You, Lord; with which they have mocked the footsteps of Your anointed one.

52 Lord, blessed are You forever more. Amen, and Amen.

PP 90 PP 90

1 Lord, You are my dwelling place, and for all my future generations.

2 Before the mountains were born, before You formed the earth and the world, even from everlasting to everlasting, You were, and are, God.

3 You turn man back to dust, saying, "Return to dust, you children of men."

4 For a thousand years in Your sight are like a day when it is past, like a watch in the night.

5 You sweep men away as they die. In the morning they sprout like new grass.

6 In the morning it sprouts and springs up. By evening, it is withered and dry.

7 For I am consumed in Your anger. I am troubled in Your wrath.

8 You set my iniquities before You; my secret sins in the light of Your presence.

9 For all my days pass away in Your wrath. My years end with a sigh.

10 The days of my years are seventy, or even by reason of strength eighty years. Yet the best of my years are labor and sorrow, for they pass quickly, and I fly away.

11 I know the power of Your anger; Your wrath according to the fear that is due to You.

12 You teach me to count my days, and I gain a heart of wisdom.

13 But You relent, Lord! You have compassion on me, Your servant!

14 You satisfy me in the morning with Your loving kindness, that I may rejoice and be glad all my days.

15 You make me glad for as many days as You afflict me, for as many years as I am distressed.

16 You make Your work apparent to me, Your servant; Your glory to my children.

17 Your favor, Lord my God, is on me. You establish the work of my hands. Yes, You establish the work of my hands.

1 Because I dwell in Your shelter, Lord Most High, I rest in Your shadow, Lord Almighty.

2 I say to You, Lord, "You are my refuge and my fortress; my God, in whom I trust."

3 You deliver me from the snare of the fowler, and from the deadly pestilence.

4 You cover me with Your feathers. Under Your wings I take refuge. Your faithfulness is my shield and rampart.

5 I am not afraid of the terror by night, nor of the arrow that flies by day,

6 nor of the pestilence that stalks in darkness, nor of the destruction that destroys at noonday.

7 A thousand may fall at my side, ten thousand at my right hand, but it does not come near me.

8 I only look with my eyes and see the punishment of the wicked.

9 Because I make You, Lord, my refuge, and You, the Most High, my dwelling place,

10 no evil comes to me, neither does any plague come near my dwelling.

11 For You put Your angels in charge of me, to guard me in all my ways.

12 They bear me up in their hands, so that I do not dash my foot against a stone.

13 I tread on the lion and cobra. I trample the strong lion and the serpent underfoot.

14 Lord, You say: "Because he has set his love on Me, therefore I deliver him. I set him on high, because he knows My name.

15 He calls on Me, and I answer him. I am with him in trouble. I deliver him and honor him.

16 I will satisfy him with long life and show him My salvation."

PP 92 PP 92

1 It is a good thing to give You thanks, Lord; to sing praises to Your name, Most High,

2 to proclaim Your loving kindness in the morning, and Your faithfulness every night,

3 with the melody of the ten-stringed lyre, and the harp.

4 For You make me glad through Your work. I triumph in the works of Your hands.

5 How great are Your works, Lord! Your thoughts are very deep.

6 A senseless man does not know, neither does a fool understand this:

7 though the wicked spring up as the grass, and all the evildoers flourish, they are destroyed forever.

8 You, Lord, are on high forever more.

9 For behold, Your enemies perish. All the evildoers are scattered.

10 But You exalt my horn like that of the wild ox. I am anointed with fresh oil.

11 My eye sees my enemies. My ear hears of the wicked enemies who rise up against me.

12 But because I am righteous in Your sight, I flourish like the palm tree. I grow like a cedar in Lebanon.

13 I am planted in Your house, Lord. I flourish in Your courts; my God's courts.

14 I still produce fruit in my old age. I am fresh and green.

15 I say of You, Lord: "You are upright. You are my rock, and there is no unrighteousness in You."

PP 93 PP 93

1 You, O Lord, reign! You are clothed with majesty! You are armed with strength. You surely established the world. It cannot be moved.

2 Your throne is established from long ago. You are from everlasting.

3 The waters rise up and lift up their voice. The waters lift up their waves.

4 Above the voices of many waters, the mighty breakers of the sea, You, Lord on High, are mighty.

5 Your statutes stand firm. Holiness adorns Your house forever more.

1 Vengeance belongs to You, Lord God. Because You avenge, You shine out.

2 You rise up because You are judge of the earth. You pay back to the proud what they deserve.

3 Lord, how long will the wicked triumph?

4 They pour out arrogant words. All the evildoers boast.

5 They break Your people in pieces, Lord, and afflict Your heritage.

6 They kill the widow and the alien and murder the fatherless.

7 They say, "The Lord will not see, neither will He consider our evil deeds."

8 Consider your deeds, you senseless people; you fools, when will you be wise?

9 Lord, You who implanted the ear, hear. You who formed the eye, see.

10 You, who disciplines the nations, punish. You, who teaches man, know all things.

11 You know the thoughts of man, that they are futile.

12 Blessed am I because You discipline me, Lord, and teach me Your law,

13 that You may give me rest from my days of adversity, until the pit is dug for the wicked.

14 For You do not reject me, neither do You forsake Your inheritance.

15 Judgement returns to me because I am righteous. All the upright in heart follow righteousness.

16 Who rises up for me against the wicked? Who stands up for me against the evildoers?

17 Lord, because You are my help, my soul does not live in the silence of death.

18 When I say, "My foot is slipping!" Your loving kindness holds me up.

19 In the multitude of my thoughts within me, Your comfort delights my soul.

20 The throne of wickedness, which brings about heartache by its deeds, does not have fellowship with You.

21 My enemies gather themselves together against my soul because I am righteous, and they condemn my innocent blood.

22 But You, Lord, are my high tower, my God, the rock of my refuge.

23 You bring on them their own iniquity and cut them off in their own wickedness. You, Lord, my God, cut them off.

PP 95

PP 95

1 Lord, I sing to You. I shout aloud to You, the rock of my salvation!

2 I come before Your presence with thanksgiving. I praise You with songs!

3 For You, Lord, are a great God; a great King above all gods.

4 In Your hand are the deep places of the earth. The heights of the mountains are also Yours.

5 The sea is Yours, for You made it. Your hands formed the dry lands.

6 I worship and bow down. I kneel before You, Lord, my Maker,

7 for You are my God. I am of the people of Your pasture, and the sheep in Your care. Today, I hear Your voice!

8 I do not harden my heart, as at Meribah, as in the day of Massah in the wilderness,

9 when my fathers tempted You, tested You, even though they saw Your amazing work.

10 Forty long years You were grieved with that generation, and said, "It is a people that errs in their heart. They have not known My ways."

11 Therefore You swore in Your wrath, "They will not enter into My rest."

PP 96 PP 96

PP 96

1 I sing a new song to You, Lord! With all the earth, I sing to You.

2 I sing to You, Lord! I bless Your name! I proclaim Your salvation from day to day!

3 I declare Your glory among the nations; Your marvelous works among all the peoples.

4 For You are great, and greatly to be praised! You are feared above all gods.

5 For all the gods of the peoples are idols, but You, Lord, made the heavens.

6 Honor and majesty are before You. Strength and beauty are in Your sanctuary.

7 With the families of nations, I ascribe glory and strength to You.

8 I ascribe to You the glory due to Your name. I bring an offering and come into Your courts.

9 I worship You in Your holiness. With all the earth, I tremble before You.

10 I say among the nations, "You, Lord, reign." You firmly established the world. It cannot be moved. You judge the peoples with equity.

11 The heavens and the earth rejoice. The sea roars, with all its fullness!

12 The field and all that is in it glorify You, Lord! All the trees of the woods sing for joy

13 before You, for You come to judge the earth. You judge the world with righteousness, and the peoples with Your truth.

1 You, Lord, reign! All the earth rejoices! The multitude of lands are glad!

2 Clouds and darkness are around You. Righteousness and justice are the foundation of Your throne.

3 A fire goes before You and burns up Your adversaries on every side.

4 Your lightning lights up the world. The earth sees and trembles.

5 The mountains melt like wax at Your presence for You are Lord of the whole earth.

6 The heavens declare Your righteousness. All the peoples see Your glory.

7 All who serve engraved images are shamed; those who boast in their idols. All of these "gods" worship You, Lord!

8 Zion hears and is glad. The daughters of Judah rejoice because of Your judgments, Lord.

9 For You are most high above all the earth. You are exalted far above all gods.

10 I love You, Lord, and hate evil! You preserve my soul and the souls of all Your saints. You deliver me out of the hand of the wicked.

11 Light shines on me because I am righteous, and I am glad for I am upright in heart.

12 With all righteous people, I rejoice in You, Lord! I give thanks to Your holy name.

PP 98
PP 98

1 Lord, I sing to You a new song, for You do marvelous things! Your right hand and Your holy arm work salvation for You.

2 You make known Your salvation. You openly show Your righteousness in the sight of the nations.

3 You remember Your loving kindness and Your faithfulness toward the house of Israel. All the ends of the earth see Your salvation.

4 With all the earth, I make a joyful noise to You! I burst out and sing for joy. Yes, I sing Your praises!

5 I sing praises to You, Lord, with the harp; with the harp and the voice of melody.

6 With trumpets and the sound of the ram's horn, I make a joyful noise before You, the King, my Lord.

7 The sea roars with its fullness, along with the world and those who dwell therein.

8 The rivers clap their hands. The mountains sing for joy together.

9 They sing before You, Lord, for You come to judge the earth. You judge the world with righteousness, and the peoples with equity.

1 You, Lord, reign! The peoples of the nations tremble. You sit enthroned among the cherubim. The earth shakes.

2 You are great in Zion. You are high above all the peoples of the nations.

3 All the people praise Your great and awesome name. You are holy!

4 In Your strength, my King, my God, You love justice. You establish equity. You execute justice and righteousness in Jacob.

5 I exalt You, my God. I worship at Your footstool. You are holy!

6 Moses and Aaron were among Your priests. Samuel was among those who called on Your name. They called on You and You answered them.

7 You spoke to them in the pillar of cloud. They kept Your testimonies and the commandments that You gave them.

8 You answered them, Lord, my God. You forgave them, although You took vengeance for their wrong doings.

9 I exalt You, Lord, my God. I worship at Your holy hill, for You, my God, are holy!

1 With all the lands, I shout for joy to You, Lord!

2 I serve You with gladness. I come before Your presence with singing.

3 I know that You are God. It is You who made me, and I am Yours. I am Yours, one of the sheep of Your pasture.

4 I enter Your gates with thanksgiving, and Your courts with praise. I give You thanks and bless Your name

5 for You are good. Your loving kindness endures forever, Your faithfulness to all generations.

1 Lord, I sing of Your loving kindness and justice. To You, I sing praises.

2 I am careful to live a blameless life, so You come to me. With a blameless heart, I walk within my house.

3 I set no vile thing before my eyes. I hate the deeds of faithless men. They do not cling to me.

4 A perverse heart is far from me. I have nothing to do with evil.

5 I silence whoever secretly slanders his neighbor. I do not tolerate one who is arrogant and conceited.

6 My eyes are on the faithful of the land, that they may dwell with me. He who walks in a righteous way ministers to me.

7 He who practices deceit does not dwell within my house. He who speaks lies does not stand before me.

8 Morning by morning, I destroy all the wicked of the land. I cut off all the workers of iniquity from Your city, Lord.

PP 102 PP 102

1 Lord, You hear my prayer! My cry for help comes to You.

2 You do not hide Your face from me in the day of my distress. You turn Your ear to me. You answer me quickly in the day when I call.

3 For my days disappear like smoke. My bones are burned as a torch.

4 My heart is blighted like grass, and withered, and I forget to eat my bread.

5 Because of my groaning, I am skin and bones.

6 I am like an owl in the wilderness. I have become as an owl in the destroyed places.

7 I watch and have become like a sparrow that is alone on the housetop.

8 My enemies insult me all day. Those who hate me use my name as a curse.

9 I eat ashes like bread and mix my drink with tears,

10 because of Your indignation and Your wrath. You take me up and throw me away.

11 My days are like a long shadow. I wither like the grass.

12 But You, Lord, remain forever; Your renown endures to all generations.

13 You arise and have mercy on me and Zion, for it is time to have pity on us. Yes, the set time has come.

14 For Your servants take pleasure in her stones and have pity on her dust.

15 The nations fear Your name. All the kings of the earth celebrate Your glory.

16 For You, Lord, build up Zion. You appear in Your glory.

17 You respond to my prayer because I am destitute. You do not despise my prayer.

18 This is written for a generation to come. A people yet to be created will praise You, Lord,

19 for You look down from the height of Your sanctuary. From heaven, You see the earth.

20 You hear my groans because I am a prisoner. You free me even though I am condemned to death.

21 Men declare Your name in Zion and Your praise in Jerusalem,

22 when all the peoples and the kingdoms are gathered together to serve You, Lord.

23 But You weaken my strength as I run my course. You shorten my days.

24 I say to You, "My God, do not take me away in the middle of my days. Your years are throughout all generations.

25 You laid the foundations of the earth. The heavens are the work of Your hands.

26 They will perish, but You will endure. Yes, all of them will wear out like a garment. You will change them like a cloak, and they will be changed.

27 But You are the same. Your years have no end.

28 The children of Your servants will continue. Their offspring are established before You."

PP 103 PP 103

1 My soul praises You, Lord! All that is within me, praises Your holy name!

2 My soul praises You and does not forget all Your benefits.

3 You forgive all my sins. You heal all my diseases.

4 You redeem my life from destruction. You crown me with loving kindness and tender mercies.

5 You satisfy my desire with good things, so that my youth is renewed like the eagle's.

6 Lord, You execute righteousness and justice for me because I am oppressed.

7 You made known Your ways to Moses; Your deeds to the children of Israel.

8 You are merciful and gracious, slow to anger, and abundant in loving kindness.

9 You do not accuse forever; neither do You stay angry forever.

10 You do not deal with me according to my sins, nor repay me for my iniquities.

11 For as the heavens are high above the earth, so great is Your loving kindness toward me because I fear You.

12 As far as the east is from the west, so far have You removed my transgressions from me.

13 Like a father has compassion on his children, so You, Lord, have compassion on me because I fear You.

14 For You know how I am made. You remember that I am dust.

15 As for me, my days are like grass. As a flower of the field, so I flourish.

16 For the wind passes over it, and it is gone. Its place remembers it no more.

17 But Your loving kindness is from everlasting to everlasting with me, because I fear You. Your righteousness endures to my children's children,

18 because I keep Your covenant and remember to obey Your teachings.

19 You establish Your throne in the heavens. Your kingdom rules over all.

20 With Your angels, I praise You, Lord. They are mighty in strength and fulfill Your word, obeying the voice of Your word.

21 I praise You with all Your armies; Your servants who do Your pleasure.

22 I praise You with all Your works, in all places of Your dominion. My soul praises You, Lord!

PP 104

PP 104

1 Lord, my soul blesses You. You, my God, You are very great. You are clothed with honor and majesty.

2 You cover Yourself with light as with a garment. You stretch out the heavens like a curtain.

3 You lay the beams of Your rooms in the waters. You make the clouds Your chariot. You walk on the wings of the wind.

4 You make winds Your messengers, and flames of fire Your servants.

5 You laid the foundations of the earth, and they shall never be moved.

6 You covered the earth with the deep as with a cloak. The waters stood above the mountains.

7 At Your rebuke the waters fled. At the voice of Your thunder they hurried away.

8 The mountains rose; the valleys sank down to the place which You had assigned to them.

9 You set a boundary that they may not pass over, that they will never again cover the earth.

10 You send springs of water into the valleys. They run among the mountains.

11 They give drink to every animal of the field. The wild donkeys quench their thirst.

12 The birds of the sky nest by them. They sing among the branches.

13 You water the mountains from Your heavenly rooms. The earth is filled with the fruit of Your works.

14 You cause the grass to grow for the livestock, and plants for me to cultivate, that I may produce food out of the earth;

15 wine that makes my heart glad, oil to make my face to shine, and bread that strengthens my heart.

16 Lord, Your trees are well watered, the cedars of Lebanon, which You planted,

17 where the birds make their nests. The stork makes its home in the cypress trees.

18 The high mountains are for the wild goats. The rocks are a refuge for the rock badgers.

19 You appointed the moon for seasons. The sun knows when to set.

20 You make darkness and it is night, in which all the animals of the forest prowl.

21 The young lions roar after their prey and seek their food from You, God.

22 The sun rises, and they steal away, and lie down in their dens.

23 I go out to my work and I labor until the evening.

24 Lord, Your works are many! In wisdom, You made them all. The earth is full of Your riches.

25 There is the sea, great and wide, in which are innumerable living things; both small and large animals.

26 There the ships go and leviathan, whom You formed to play there.

27 These all wait for You that You may give them their food in due season.

28 You give to them and they gather it. You open Your hand and they are satisfied with good.

29 You hide Your face and they are troubled. You take away their breath and they die and return to the dust.

30 You send out Your Spirit and they are created. You renew the face of the earth.

31 Lord, Your glory endures forever. You rejoice in Your works.

32 You look at the earth and it trembles. You touch the mountains and they smoke.

33 Lord, I sing to You as long as I live. I sing praise to You, my God, while I have any breath.

34 May my meditation be pleasing to You. I rejoice in You.

35 You consume sinners out of the earth. The wicked are no more. My soul blesses You, Lord. I Praise You!

1 God, I give You thanks! I call on Your name! I make all Your deeds known among the peoples.

2 I sing to You; I sing praises to You, Lord! I tell of all Your marvelous works.

3 I glory in Your holy name. My heart rejoices, along with all of those who seek You.

4 I seek You and Your strength. I seek Your face forever.

5 I remember Your marvelous works; Your wonders and the judgments of Your mouth, along with all

6 the offspring of Abraham, Your servant; the children of Jacob, Your chosen ones.

7 You are God, my God. Your judgments are on all the earth.

8 You remember Your covenant forever; the word which You command to a thousand generations;

9 the covenant which You made with Abraham; Your oath to Isaac.

10 You confirmed it to Jacob as a statute; to Israel as an everlasting covenant,

11 saying, "To you I will give the land of Canaan, the lot of your inheritance,"

12 when they were but a few men in number, yes, very few, and foreigners in the land.

13 They went about from nation to nation, from one kingdom to another.

14 You allowed no one to do them wrong. Yes, You defeated kings for their sakes, saying,

15 "Do not touch My anointed ones! Do My prophets no harm!"

16 You called for a famine on the land. You destroyed the food supplies.

17 You sent a man before them, Joseph, who was sold as a slave.

18 They bruised his feet with shackles. His neck was locked in irons,

19 until the time that Your word was fulfilled, that was foretold by Joseph; and Your word, Lord, proved him true.

20 The king, the pharaoh, even the ruler of peoples, sent and freed Joseph, and let him go free.

21 He made Joseph lord of pharaoh's house, and ruler of all of the king's possessions,

22 to discipline the king's princes at his pleasure, and to teach pharaoh's elders wisdom.

23 Then Israel also came into Egypt. Jacob lived in the land of Ham.

24 God, You increased Your people greatly, and made them stronger than their adversaries.

25 You turned pharaoh's heart to hate Your people, to conspire against Your servants.

26 You sent Moses, Your servant, and Aaron, whom You chose.

27 They performed Your miracles among the Egyptians, and Your wonders in the land of Ham.

28 You sent darkness and made it dark. For the Egyptians rebelled against Your words.

29 You turned their waters into blood and killed their fish.

30 Their land swarmed with frogs, even in the rooms of their kings.

31 You spoke and swarms of flies came, and gnats throughout their borders.

32 You gave them hail for rain, with lightning in their land.

33 You struck their vines and also their fig trees and shattered the trees of their country.

34 You spoke and the locusts came with the grasshoppers, too many to number.

35 They ate up every plant in the Egyptian's land, and ate up the fruit of their ground.

36 You also struck all the firstborn in their land, the first fruits of all their manhood.

37 You brought all of Israel out with silver and gold. There was not one feeble person among Your tribes.

38 Egypt was glad when the Hebrews departed, for the fear of them had fallen on all the peoples.

39 You spread a cloud for a covering and a pillar of fire to give light in the night.

40 They asked and You brought quails, and You satisfied them with the bread of heaven, manna.

41 You opened the rock and waters gushed out. They ran as a river in the dry places.

42 For You remember Your holy word and Abraham, Your servant.

43 You brought Your people out with joy, Your chosen with singing.

44 You gave them the lands of the nations. They took the possessions of the peoples in the lands,

45 that they might keep Your statutes and observe Your laws. I praise You, Lord!

PP 106 PP 106

1 God, I praise You! I give thanks to You, for You are good. Your loving kindness endures forever.

2 I declare Your mighty acts, Lord, and fully declare all Your praise.

3 I am blessed because I keep justice. I am blessed because I do what is right at all times.

4 You remember me, Lord, with the favor that You show to Your people. You visit me with Your salvation.

5 I see prosperity, as one of Your chosen. I rejoice in the gladness of Your nation. I glory along with Your inheritance.

6 But, I have sinned with my fathers. I have committed iniquity. I have done wickedly.

7 My fathers did not understand Your wonders in Egypt. They did not remember the multitude of Your loving kindnesses, but were rebellious at the sea, even at the Red Sea.

8 Nevertheless, You saved them for Your name's sake, that You should make Your mighty power known.

9 You rebuked the Red Sea and it was dried up. You led them through the depths, as through a desert.

10 You saved Your people from the hand of pharaoh who hated them. You redeemed them from the hand of their enemy.

11 But, the waters covered their pursuers. Not one of them was left.

12 Then my fathers believed Your words. They sang Your praise.

13 But they soon forgot Your works. They did not wait for Your counsel,

14 but gave in to cravings in the desert. They tested You, God, in the wasteland.

15 You gave them their request, but sent deadly disease into their midst.

16 They envied Moses in the camp, and Aaron, Your consecrated servant.

17 The earth opened and swallowed up Dathan and covered the company of Abiram.

18 A fire was kindled in their company. The flame burned up the wicked.

19 They made a calf in Horeb and worshiped the formed metal image.

20 Yes, they exchanged Your Glory for an image of a bull that eats grass.

21 They forgot You, their Savior, who had done great things in Egypt;

22 wondrous works in the land of Ham, and awesome things by the Red Sea.

23 Therefore, You said that You would destroy them. But Moses, Your chosen, stood before You in the breach, to turn away Your wrath. Thus, You did not destroy them.

24 They despised the pleasant, promised land and did not believe Your word.

25 They murmured in their tents, and did not listen to Your voice, Lord.

26 Therefore, You swore to them that You would overthrow them in the wilderness;

27 that You would disperse their offspring among the nations and scatter them in the lands.

28 They joined themselves to Baal Peor, and ate the sacrifices offered to lifeless idols.

29 They provoked You to anger with their deeds. Thus, a plague overtook them.

30 But Phinehas stood up and executed judgment, so the plague was stopped.

31 You credited that to him as righteousness, for all generations to come.

32 Your people angered You at the waters of Meribah, bringing trouble on Moses because of them.

33 Because they were rebellious against Your spirit, Moses spoke rashly with his lips.

34 They did not destroy the peoples of the pleasant, promised land, as You commanded them to do,

35 but intermingled themselves with those nations and learned their cultures and ways.

36 Your people served their idols, which became a snare to them.

37 Yes, Your people sacrificed their sons and their daughters to demons.

38 They shed innocent blood, even the blood of their sons and of their daughters, whom they sacrificed to the idols of Canaan. The land was polluted with blood.

39 Thus they were defiled by their actions and prostituted themselves in their deeds.

40 Therefore You, Lord, burned with anger against Your people. You abhorred Your inheritance.

41 You gave them into the hands of the nations. Those who hated them ruled over them.

42 Their enemies oppressed them. They were brought into subjection under their enemy's hand.

43 You rescued them many times, but they were determined to rebel against You. They were brought low in their sins.

44 But You took note of their distress, when You heard their cry.

45 You remembered Your covenant for their sake and relented according to the multitude of Your loving kindnesses.

46 You also made them to be pitied by all those who had captured them.

47 You save us, Lord, my God, and gather us from among the nations. We give thanks to Your holy name. We triumph in Your praise!

48 Blessed are You, the God of Israel, from everlasting to everlasting! With all the people, I say, "Amen." I praise You, Lord!

PP 107 PP 107

1 God, I give You thanks, for You are good. Your loving kindness endures forever.

2 I say these things because You redeem me, along with all those that You redeem from the hand of the enemy.

3 You gather me out of the lands, from the east and from the west, from the north and from the south.

4 I wander in the wilderness; in the desert. I find no city to live in.

5 Hungry and thirsty, my soul faints away.

6 But I cry to You, Lord, in my trouble, and You deliver me out of my distresses.

7 You lead me by a straight way, that I might go to a city to live in.

8 I praise You, Lord, for Your loving kindness; for Your wonderful deeds to me and the children of men!

9 For You satisfy my longing soul. You fill my hungry soul with good.

10 Some sit in darkness and in the shadow of death, being bound in affliction and iron,

11 because they rebel against Your words and condemn Your counsel, Lord, Most High.

12 Therefore You bring down their heart with labor. They fall down, and there is no one to help.

13 But they cry to You, Lord, in their trouble, and You save them out of their distresses.

14 You bring them out of darkness and the shadow of death and break away their chains.

15 Now we all praise You for Your loving kindness, for Your wonderful deeds to the children of men!

16 You break the gates of bronze and cut through bars of iron.

17 Fools are afflicted because of their disobedience, and because of their iniquities.

18 In their affliction, they abhor all kinds of food. They draw near to the gates of death.

19 But they cry to You in their trouble, and You save them out of their distresses.

20 You send Your word, and heal them, and deliver them from their graves.

21 Now we all praise You, Lord, for Your loving kindness, for Your wonderful deeds to the children of men!

22 We offer the sacrifices of thanksgiving and declare Your deeds with singing.

23 Those who go down to the sea in ships, who do business in great waters,

24 see Your deeds, and Your wonders in the deep.

25 For You command, and raise the stormy wind, which lifts up its waves.

26 The seas mount up to the sky; they go down again to the depths. In their ships, their courage melts away because of trouble.

27 They reel back and forth, and stagger like a drunken man, and are at their wits' end.

28 But they cry to You, Lord, in their trouble, and You bring them out of their distress.

29 You calm the storm and still its waves.

30 Then they are glad because the sea is calm. You bring them to their desired safe destination.

31 Now we all praise You, Lord, for Your loving kindness, for Your wonderful deeds for the children of men!

32 We exalt You in the assembly of the people and praise You in the seat of the elders.

33 You turn rivers into a desert. You turn flowing springs into a dry thirsty ground.

34 You turn a fruitful land into a salt waste, because of the wickedness of those who dwell in it.

35 You turn a desert into a pool of water, and a dry land into watery springs.

36 There You brought the hungry to live, that they may prepare a city to live in,

37 sow fields, plant vineyards, and reap the fruits of increase.

38 You also bless them, so that they are multiplied greatly. You do not allow their livestock to decrease.

39 Again, they are diminished and bowed down through oppression, trouble, and sorrow.

40 You pour contempt on princes and cause them to wander in a trackless waste.

41 Yet You lift the needy out of their affliction and increase their families like a flock.

42 Because I am upright in Your sight, I see it and am glad. But all the wicked shut their mouths.

43 Because I am wise, I pay attention to these things. I consider Your loving kindnesses, Lord.

PP 108

1 God, my heart is steadfast. I sing and make music with my soul.

2 With the harp and lyre, I wake up the dawn!

3 Lord, I give thanks to You among the nations. I sing Your praises among the peoples.

4 For Your loving kindness is great above the heavens. Your faithfulness reaches to the skies.

5 I exalt You, God, above the heavens! Your glory covers all the earth.

6 I am delivered because I am Your beloved. You save me with Your right hand, and You answer me.

7 You speak from Your sanctuary: "In triumph, I will divide Shechem, and measure out the valley of Succoth.

8 Gilead is mine. Manasseh is mine. Ephraim also is my helmet. Judah is my scepter.

9 Moab is my wash pot. I will toss my sandal on Edom. I will shout over Philistia."

10 You bring me into Your fortified city. You lead me to Edom.

11 But You have rejected me, God, and You do not go out with my armies.

12 Still, You give me help against my enemy, for the help of man is useless.

13 Through You I perform valiantly, for it is You who treads down my enemies.

1 God of my praise, You do not remain silent,

2 for my enemies open their mouths with wickedness and deceit against me. They speak about me with a lying tongue.

3 They surround me with words of hatred, and fight against me without cause.

4 In return for my love, they are my adversaries. But, I am a man of prayer.

5 They reward me evil for good and hatred for my love.

6 But, Lord, You set an evil man to oppose my enemy. You make an adversary stand at his right hand.

7 When You judge him, You find him guilty. You turn his prayer against him.

8 You make his days be few. You let another take his office.

9 You make his children be fatherless, and his wife a widow.

10 You make his children be wandering beggars. You drive them from their homes.

11 You make the creditor seize all that he has. You make strangers plunder the fruit of his labor.

12 You remove anyone who would extend kindness to him or have pity on his fatherless children.

13 You cut off his children. You blot out their names from future generations.

14 Lord, You remember the iniquity of his fathers. You do not blot out the sin of his mother.

15 Their sin is continually before You that You may cut off their memory from the earth;

16 because he does not show kindness, but persecutes the poor and needy man, the broken in heart, to kill them.

17 Because he loves cursing, You make the curses come back to him. He does not delight in blessings, so You keep blessings far from him.

18 He clothes himself with cursing as a garment. It comes into his inward parts like water, like oil into his bones.

19 You make it be to him as the clothing with which he covers himself; the belt that is always around him.

20 This is the reward for my adversaries from You, Lord; for those who speak evil against me.

21 But You deal kindly with me, God, for Your name's sake. Because Your loving kindness is good, You deliver me,

22 for I am poor and needy. My heart is wounded within me.

23 I fade away like an evening shadow. I am shaken off like a locust.

24 My knees are weak from fasting. My body is thin and lacks fat.

25 I have become a reproach to my enemies. When they see me, they shake their head.

26 But You help me, Lord. You save me according to Your loving kindness,

27 that my enemies may know that this is Your hand; that You, Lord, accomplish it.

28 My enemies curse, but You bless. When they arise, You cause them to be shamed. But I rejoice because I am Your servant.

29 You clothe my adversaries with dishonor. You cover them with their own shame as with a robe.

30 I give great thanks to You, Lord, with my mouth. Yes, I praise You among the multitude.

31 For You stand at my right hand because I am needy. You save me from those who judge my soul.

PP 110 PP 110

1 God, You say to my Lord, "Sit at My right hand, until I make Your enemies Your footstool for Your feet."

2 You send out the rod of Your strength from Zion. You rule among Your enemies.

3 Your warriors offer themselves willingly in the day when You show Your power; in Your holy array. Out of the womb of the morning, You bring the dew of Your youth.

4 You have sworn and will not change Your mind: "You are a priest forever in the order of Melchizedek."

5 You, Lord, are at my right hand. You crush kings in the day of Your wrath.

6 You judge among the nations. You heap up dead bodies. You crush the rulers of the whole earth.

7 You drink of the brook on Your way; therefore, You lift up Your head.

——— PP 111

1 Lord, I praise You! I give thanks to You with my whole heart, in the council of the upright, and in the congregation.

2 Your works are great, pondered by all those who delight in them.

3 Your work is honor and majesty. Your righteousness endures forever.

4 You cause Your wonderful works to be remembered. You, Lord, are gracious and merciful.

5 You give food to those who fear You. You always remember Your covenant.

6 You show Your people the power of Your works by giving them the lands of the nations.

7 The works of Your hands are truth and justice. All Your teachings are sure.

8 They are established forever and ever. They are done in truth and uprightness.

9 You send redemption to Your people. You ordain Your covenant forever. Your name is holy and awesome!

10 Lord, the fear of You is the beginning of wisdom. All those who do Your work have a good understanding. Your praise endures forever!

1 Lord, I praise You! Blessed am I because I fear You and delight greatly in Your commandments.

2 My offspring are mighty in the land. The generation of the upright are blessed.

3 Wealth and riches are in my house. My righteousness endures forever.

4 Light dawns in the darkness for me because I am upright, gracious, merciful, and righteous.

5 It is well with me because I deal graciously and lend. I conduct my affairs with justice.

6 I am never shaken. Because I am righteous, I am remembered forever.

7 I am not afraid of evil news. My heart is steadfast, trusting in You, Lord.

8 My heart is established in security. I am not afraid. In the end, I have victory over my adversaries.

9 I give widely and generously to the poor. My righteousness endures forever. My horn is exalted with honor.

10 The wicked see it and are grieved. They gnash their teeth and melt away. The desires of the wicked perish.

PP 113

1 Along with all Your servants, I praise You, Lord! I praise Your name.

2 Blessed is Your name from this time forward and forever more.

3 From the rising of the sun, to its going down, I praise Your name.

4 Lord, You are high above all nations. Your glory is above the heavens.

5 Who is like You, my God, who sits on high,

6 who stoops down to see into heaven and into the earth?

7 You raise up the poor out of the dust, and lift up the needy from the ash heap,

8 that You may set him with princes, even with the princes of Your people.

9 You settle the barren woman in her home as a joyful mother of children. I praise You, Lord!

PP 114

1 When Israel went out of Egypt, the house of Jacob from a people of foreign language,

2 Judah became Your sanctuary, God; Israel Your dominion.

3 The sea saw it and fled. The Jordan was driven back.

4 The mountains skipped like rams, the little hills like lambs.

5 What was it, that made you oceans flee? What turned you back Jordan?

6 You mountains, what made you skip like rams; you little hills, like lambs?

7 The earth trembles at Your presence, Lord; at the presence of the God of Jacob.

8 Lord, You turn the rock into a pool of water; the solid rock into a spring of waters.

PP 115

PP 115

1 Not to me, Lord, not to me, but to Your name is the glory, for Your loving kindness and for Your truth's sake.

2 Why should the nations say of me, "Where is his God, now?"

3 But You, my God, are in the heavens. You do whatever pleases You.

4 The nation's idols are silver and gold, the work of men's hands.

5 They have mouths, but they do not speak. They have eyes, but they do not see.

6 They have ears, but they do not hear. They have noses, but they do not smell.

7 They have hands, but they do not feel. They have feet, but they do not walk, neither do they make a sound through their throat.

8 Those who make them are like them; yes, and everyone who trusts in them.

9 With Israel, I trust in You, Lord! You are my help and my shield.

10 With the house of Aaron, I trust in You! You are my help and my shield.

11 Because I fear You, I also trust in You! You are my help and my shield.

12 You remember me and bless me. You bless the house of Israel. You bless the house of Aaron.

13 You bless me because I fear You. You bless both the small and the great.

14 God, You increase me more and more; me and my children.

15 Blessed am I by You, Lord, who made heaven and earth.

16 The heavens are Your heavens, but You have given the earth to the children of men.

17 The dead do not praise You, nor do any who go down into silence,

18 but I bless You, from this time forward and forever more. I praise You!

PP 116 PP 116

1 Lord, I love You because You listen to my voice and hear my cries for mercy.

2 Because You turn Your ear to me, I call on You always.

3 The cords of death surround me, and the pains of the grave get a hold on me. I find trouble and sorrow.

4 Then I call on Your name: "Lord, I beg You, deliver my soul."

5 You are gracious and righteous. Yes, You are merciful.

6 You preserve me because I am simple-hearted. I am brought low and You save me.

7 My soul returns to rest, for You deal bountifully with me.

8 You deliver my soul from death, my eyes from tears, and my feet from falling.

9 I walk before You in the land of the living.

10 I believe; therefore, I say, "I am greatly afflicted."

11 In my disappointment, I say, "All people are liars."

12 I can never repay You, Lord, for all Your benefits toward me.

13 I take the cup of salvation and call on Your name.

14 I pay my vows to You; yes, in the presence of all Your people.

15 Precious in Your sight is the death of Your saints.

16 Lord, truly I am Your servant. I am Your servant, the son of Your servant girl. You have freed me from my chains.

17 I offer to You the sacrifice of thanksgiving and call on Your name.

18 I pay my vows to You; yes, in the presence of all Your people.

19 In the courts of Your house, in the middle of Jerusalem. I praise You!

PP 117   PP 117

1 Along with all the nations, I praise You, Lord! With all the peoples, I exalt You!

2 For Your loving kindness is great toward me. Your faithfulness endures forever. I praise You!

PP 118   PP 118

1 Lord, I give You thanks, for You are good. Your loving kindness endures forever.

2 With Israel, I declare that Your loving kindness endures forever.

3 With the house of Aaron, I declare that Your loving kindness endures forever.

4 Because I fear You, I declare that Your loving kindness endures forever.

5 Out of my distress, I call on You and You answer me with freedom for my life.

6 You are by my side, so I am not afraid. What can man do to me?

7 Lord, You are by my side; You help me. Therefore, I look triumphantly at those who hate me.

8 God, it is better to take refuge in You, than to put confidence in man.

9 It is better to take refuge in You, than to put confidence in princes.

10 All the nations surround me, but in Your name, I cut them off.

11 They surround me; yes, they surround me. In Your name I indeed cut them off.

12 They surround me like bees but are consumed as quickly as burning thorns. In Your name I cut them off.

13 My enemy pushes me back hard, to make me fall, but You, Lord, help me.

14 You are my strength and song. You are my salvation.

15 Because I am righteous in Your sight, the voice of rejoicing and salvation is in my tents. "Lord, Your right hand performs mightily.

16 Your right hand is exalted! Your right hand performs mightily!"

17 I do not die, but live, and declare Your mighty works.

18 You have punished me severely but have not given me over to death.

19 Still, You open to me the gates of righteousness and I enter into them. I give You thanks.

20 Lord, this is Your gate; I enter into it because I am righteous.

21 I give You thanks, for You answer me, and You are my salvation.

22 The stone which the builders rejected has become the cornerstone.

23 Lord, this is Your doing and it is marvelous in my eyes.

24 This is the day that You have made. I rejoice and am glad in it!

25 I call to You, and You save me! I call to You and You send prosperity.

26 Blessed am I because I come in Your name! From Your house, Lord, I am blessed.

27 You are God, and You give me light. I bind my sacrifice with cords, even to the horns of the altar.

28 You are my God, and I give You thanks. You are my God and I exalt You.

29 I give You thanks, for You are good. Your loving kindness endures forever.

PP 119 PP 119

1 Blessed am I because my ways are blameless and I walk according to Your law, Lord.

2 Blessed am I because I keep Your statutes; because I seek You with my whole heart.

3 Yes, I do nothing wrong. I walk in Your ways.

4 You command Your teachings and I fully obey them.

5 My ways are steadfast, because I obey Your statutes!

6 I am not disappointed when I consider all of Your commandments.

7 I give You thanks with an upright heart as I learn Your righteous commandments.

8 I observe Your statutes, and You do not forsake me.

9 How do I keep my way pure? By living according to Your word.

10 With my whole heart I seek You. You do not let me wander from Your commandments.

11 I have hidden Your word in my heart, that I might not sin against You.

12 Blessed are You, Lord. You teach me Your statutes.

13 With my lips, I declare all the ordinances of Your mouth.

14 I rejoice in obeying Your commandments, like one rejoices in riches.

15 I meditate on Your teachings and learn Your ways.

16 I delight myself in Your statutes. I do not forget Your word.

17 You are good to me, Your servant. I live and I obey Your word.

18 You open my eyes, and I see wondrous things in Your law.

19 I am a stranger on the earth, but You do not hide Your commandments from me.

20 My soul is consumed with longing for Your commandments at all times.

21 You rebuke the proud who are cursed; those who wander from Your commandments.

22 But, You take reproach and contempt away from me, for I keep Your statutes.

23 Though princes sit and slander me, Your servant, I meditate on Your statutes.

24 Indeed Your statutes are my delight and my counselors.

25 My soul is laid low in the dust, but You revive me according to Your word!

26 I tell You of my ways and You answer me. You teach me Your statutes.

27 You let me understand the teaching of Your precepts! I meditate on Your wondrous works.

28 My soul is weary with sorrow, but You strengthen me according to Your word.

29 You keep me from the way of deceit. You graciously grant me Your law!

30 I choose the way of truth. I set Your ordinances before me.

31 I cling to Your statutes, Lord, and I am not disappointed.

32 I run in the path of Your commandments, for You set my heart free.

33 Lord, You teach me the way of Your statutes. I will keep them to the end.

34 You give me understanding, and I keep Your law. Yes, I obey it with my whole heart.

35 You direct me in the path of Your commandments, for I delight in them.

36 You turn my heart toward Your statutes and away from selfish gain.

37 You turn my eyes away from looking at worthless things. You preserve me in accordance with Your way.

38 You fulfill Your promise to me, Your servant, and I fear You.

39 You take away my disgrace, for Your ordinances are good.

40 Behold, I long for Your teachings! You revive me in Your righteousness.

41 You cover me with Your loving kindness, Lord; Your salvation, according to Your word.

42 I have an answer for him who accuses me, for I trust in Your word.

43 You do not snatch the word of truth out of my mouth, for I put my hope in Your commandments.

44 I obey Your law continually, forever and ever.

45 I walk in liberty, for I always seek Your teachings.

46 I speak of Your statutes before kings, and I am not shamed.

47 I delight myself in Your commandments, because I love them.

48 I reach out my hands for Your commandments, which I love. I meditate on Your statutes.

49 You remember Your word to me, Your servant, and You give me hope.

50 This is my comfort in my affliction, for Your word revives me.

51 The arrogant mock me mercilessly, but I do not swerve from Your law.

52 I remember Your ordinances from of old, Lord, and they comfort me.

53 Indignation takes hold of me, because of the wicked who forsake Your law.

54 Your statutes are my songs in the house where I live.

55 Lord, I remember Your name in the night, and I obey Your law.

56 This is my way, that I keep Your teachings.

57 Lord, You are my portion. I promise to obey Your words.

58 I seek Your favor with my whole heart. You are merciful to me according to Your word.

59 I consider my ways and turn my steps to Your statutes.

60 I hurry, and I do not delay, to obey Your commandments.

61 The ropes of the wicked bind me, but I do not forget Your law.

62 At midnight I rise to give You thanks because of Your righteous ordinances.

63 I am a friend of all those who fear You; of those who observe Your teachings.

64 The earth is full of Your loving kindness, Lord. You teach me Your statutes.

65 You treat me, Your servant, well according to Your word.

66 You teach me good judgment and knowledge, for I believe in Your commandments.

67 Before I was afflicted, and I went astray. But, now I observe Your word.

68 You are good, and You do good. You teach me Your statutes.

69 The proud smear a lie upon me. But with my whole heart, I keep Your teachings.

70 Their hearts are callous, without feeling, but I delight in Your law.

71 It is good for me that I am afflicted, for then I learn Your statutes.

72 Your law that comes from Your mouth is better to me than thousands of pieces of gold and silver.

73 Your hands made me and formed me. You give me understanding, and I learn Your commandments.

74 Those who fear You see me and are glad, because I put my hope in Your word.

75 Lord, I know that Your judgments are righteous; that in faithfulness You afflict me.

76 Your loving kindness is my comfort, according to Your word to me, Your servant.

77 Your tender mercies come to me and I live, for Your law is my delight.

78 The proud are disgraced, for they wrongfully overthrow me. But I still meditate on Your teachings.

79 Those who fear You turn to me. They know Your statutes.

80 My heart is blameless toward Your decrees, and I am not disappointed.

81 My soul does not faint waiting for Your salvation because I hope in Your word.

82 My eyes do not fail as I search Your word. I say, "You comfort me!"

83 Although I am like a wineskin in the smoke, I do not forget Your statutes.

84 I wait expectantly for You, Lord. Then You execute judgment on those who persecute me, Your servant.

85 The proud dig pits for me, contrary to Your law.

86 All of Your commandments are faithful. My enemies persecute me wrongfully, but You rescue me!

87 They almost wipe me from the earth, but I do not forsake Your teachings.

88 You preserve my life according to Your loving kindness, because I obey the statutes of Your mouth.

89 Lord, Your word is settled in heaven forever.

90 Your faithfulness is to all generations. You established the earth, and it remains.

91 Your laws remain to this day, for all things serve You.

92 Because Your law is my delight, I do not perish in my affliction.

93 I never forget Your teachings, for with them, You revive me.

94 I am Yours. You save me because I always seek Your teachings.

95 The wicked wait for me, to destroy me, but I meditate on Your statutes.

96 I see that all perfection has a limit, but Your commands are boundless.

97 How I love Your law! It is my meditation all day.

98 Your commandments make me wiser than my enemies, for Your commandments are always with me.

99 I have more understanding than all my teachers, because Your testimonies are my meditation.

100 I understand more than the aged, because I keep Your teachings.

101 I keep my feet from every evil way, and I observe Your word.

102 I do not turn away from Your ordinances, because You, Yourself, teach me.

103 How sweet are Your promises to my taste; more than honey to my mouth!

104 Through Your teachings, I get understanding; therefore, I hate every false way.

105 Your word is a lamp to my feet, and a light for my path.

106 I swear, and confirm it, that I obey Your righteous ordinances.

107 I am afflicted very much, but You revive me, Lord, according to Your word.

108 You accept the willing offerings of my mouth. You teach me Your ordinances.

109 Although I continually take my life in my own hands, I do not forget Your law.

110 The wicked lay a snare for me, yet I do not go astray from Your teachings.

111 I take Your testimonies as my possession forever, for they are the joy of my heart.

112 I set my heart to obey Your statutes forever, even to the end.

113 I hate double-minded men, but I love Your law.

114 You are my hiding place and my shield. My hope is in Your word.

115 Depart from me, you evildoers, that I may keep the commandments of my God.

116 Lord, You uphold me according to Your word, and I live. I am not ashamed because my hope is in You.

117 You hold me up, and I am safe. I respect Your statutes continually.

118 You reject all those who stray from Your statutes. Their treachery is in vain.

119 You throw out all the wicked of the earth like dross. Therefore, I love Your testimonies.

120 My flesh trembles for fear of You. I am awed by Your judgments.

121 I do what is just and righteous. Therefore, You do not leave me to my oppressors.

122 You ensure my well-being, and You do not let the proud oppress me, Your servant.

123 My eyes do not fail looking for Your salvation; for Your righteous word.

124 You deal with me, Your servant, according to Your loving kindness. You teach me Your statutes.

125 I am Your servant. You give me understanding, and I know Your testimonies.

126 It is time to act, Lord, for they break Your law.

127 I love Your commandments more than gold, yes, more than pure gold.

128 I consider all of Your teachings to be right. I hate every false way.

129 Your testimonies are wonderful, and my soul keeps them.

130 The utterance of Your words gives light. It gives understanding to the simple.

131 I open my mouth wide and pant, for I long for Your commandments.

132 You turn to me, and have mercy on me, as You always do to those who love Your name.

133 You establish my footsteps in Your word. No iniquity has dominion over me.

134 You redeem me from the oppression of man, because I observe Your teachings.

135 Your face shines on me, Your servant. You teach me Your statutes.

136 Streams of tears run down from my eyes, because people do not observe Your law.

137 You are righteous, Lord. Your judgments are upright.

138 You command Your statutes in righteousness. They are fully trustworthy.

139 My zeal wears me out, because my enemies ignore Your words.

140 Your promises are thoroughly tested, and I, Your servant, love them.

141 I am low and despised, but I do not forget Your teachings.

142 Your righteousness is an everlasting righteousness. Your law is truth.

143 Trouble and anguish take hold of me, but Your commandments are my delight.

144 Your testimonies are righteous forever. You give me understanding, and I live.

145 I call to You with my whole heart, and You answer me, Lord! I keep Your statutes.

146 I call to You, and You save me! I obey Your statutes.

147 I rise before dawn and cry to You for help. I put my hope in Your words.

148 My eyes stay open through the night watches, and I meditate on Your word.

149 You hear my voice according to Your loving kindness. You revive me, Lord, according to Your ordinances.

150 Those who chase wickedness draw near to me. They are far from Your law.

151 But, You are near, Lord. All Your commandments are truth.

152 Long ago, I learned that You established Your teachings, and they will last forever.

153 You consider my afflictions, and You deliver me, for I do not forget Your law.

154 You plead my cause, and You redeem me! You revive me according to Your promise.

155 Salvation is far from the wicked, for they do not seek Your statutes.

156 Great are Your tender mercies, Lord. You revive me according to Your ordinances.

157 Many are my persecutors and my adversaries, but I do not swerve from Your testimonies.

158 I look at the faithless with loathing, because they do not observe Your word.

159 You consider how I love Your teachings, and You revive me according to Your loving kindness.

160 All of Your words are truth. Every one of Your righteous ordinances endures forever.

161 Princes persecute me without a cause, but my heart stands in awe of Your words.

162 I rejoice at Your word, as one who finds great plunder.

163 I hate and abhor lies, but I love Your law.

164 Seven times a day, I praise You, because of Your righteous ordinances.

165 With all those who love Your law, I have great peace. Nothing causes me to stumble.

166 I hope in Your salvation, Lord. I obey Your commandments.

167 My soul observes Your testimonies. I love them exceedingly.

168 I obey Your teachings and Your testimonies, for all my ways are before You.

169 My cry comes before You. You give me understanding according to Your word.

170 My supplication comes before You. You deliver me according to Your word.

171 My lips utter Your praise, because You teach me Your statutes.

172 My tongue sings of Your word, for all Your commandments are righteousness.

173 Your hand always helps me, because I choose Your teachings.

174 I delight in Your salvation, Lord. Your law is my delight.

175 My soul lives, and I praise You. Your ordinances always help me.

176 If I go astray like a lost sheep, You seek me and You find me, Your servant, for I do not forget Your commandments.

PP 120

1 Lord, in my distress, I cry to You and You answer me.

2 You deliver my soul from lying lips; from a deceitful tongue.

3 What punishment will You give to my adversaries? What more will You do to those deceitful tongues?

4 You punish my adversaries with Your mighty arrows and with blazing coals of the juniper tree.

5 Woe is me, that I live in Meshech, that I dwell among the tents of Kedar!

6 My soul has dwelled too long with those who hate peace.

7 I am for peace, but when I speak, they are for war.

PP 121

1 I lift up my eyes to the hills, for that is where my help comes from.

2 Lord, my help comes from You, who made heaven and earth.

3 You do not allow my foot to slip. You always guard me, and You never sleep.

4 Behold, You guard Israel. You neither slumber nor sleep.

5 Lord, You are my guard and watchman. You are my shade at my right hand.

6 The sun does not harm me by day, nor the moon by night.

7 You keep me from all evil. You guard my soul.

8 Lord, You guard my going out and my coming in, from this time forward, and forever more.

PP 122

PP 122

1 I am glad when they say to me, "Let us go to the Lord's house!"

2 My feet stand within your gates, Jerusalem!

3 Jerusalem is built as a city that is built close together,

4 where the tribes go up, even Your tribes, Lord, according to Your ordinance for Israel, that they give thanks to the name of Jerusalem.

5 For the thrones for judgment, the thrones of David's house, are there.

6 I pray for the peace of Jerusalem. I prosper because I love her, along with all those who love her.

7 Peace is within your walls, and prosperity within your palaces, Jerusalem.

8 For my brothers' and companions' sakes, I say, "Peace be within you, Jerusalem."

9 For the sake of Your house, Lord, my God, I seek Jerusalem's good.

PP 123

PP 123

1 Lord, I lift up my eyes to You, where You sit in the heavens.

2 Behold, as the eyes of servants look to the hand of their master; as the eyes of a maid to the hand of her mistress, so my eyes look to You, my God, because You have mercy on me.

3 You have mercy on me, Lord. You have mercy on me, for I have endured much contempt.

4 My soul is exceedingly filled with the insults of those who are at ease, with contempt from the proud.

PP 124

PP 124

1 Lord, if You had not been on my side, I say,

2 if You had not been on my side, when men rose up against me,

3 then they would have swallowed me up alive. When their wrath was kindled against me,

4 the waters would have overwhelmed me; the stream would have gone over my soul.

5 Then the powerful waters would have gone over my soul.

6 Blessed are You, Lord, who did not give me as prey to be torn apart.

7 My soul escaped like a bird out of the fowler's snare. The snare is broken, and I escaped.

8 Lord, my help is in Your name; You who made heaven and earth.

PP 125 PP 125

1 Lord, because I trust in You, I am as Mount Zion, which cannot be shaken, but remains forever.

2 As the mountains surround Jerusalem, so You surround me from this time forward and forever more.

3 The scepter of wickedness will not remain over my allotment from You because I am righteous. Because I am righteous, I will not use my hands to do evil.

4 Lord, You do good to me because I am good; because I am upright in my heart.

5 But as for those who turn away to their crooked ways, You banish them with the workers of evil. Peace be on Israel.

PP 126 PP 126

1 Lord, when You bring me back to You, I am like those who are restored to health.

2 My mouth is filled with laughter, and my tongue with singing. Then I say among the nations, "You, Lord, do great things for me."

3 You do great things for me, and I am glad.

4 You restore my fortunes like streams in the Negev.

5 Although I may sow in tears, I reap in joy.

6 Although I may go out weeping, carrying seed for sowing, I surely come again with joy, carrying my sheaves.

PP 127 PP 127

1 Lord, unless You build the house, they who build it labor in vain. Unless You watch over the city, the watchman guards it in vain.

2 It is unproductive for me to rise up early and to stay up late eating the bread of toil; for You give me sleep as one of Your loved ones.

3 Behold, children are a heritage from You, Lord. The fruit of the womb is Your reward.

4 As arrows in the hand of a mighty man, so are the children born to me in my youth.

5 Happy am I because my quiver is full of them. I am not shamed when I speak with my enemies in the gate.

PP 128 PP 128

1 Blessed am I because I fear You, Lord, and walk in Your ways.

2 For I eat the labor of my hands. I am happy, and all is well with me.

3 My wife is as a fruitful vine in my house; my children like olive shoots around my table.

4 Behold, this is how I am blessed because I fear You, Lord.

5 You bless me from Zion, and I see the success of Jerusalem all the days of my life.

6 Yes, I live to see my children's children. Peace be upon Israel.

PP 129 PP 129

1 Many times my enemies have afflicted me from my youth; I say:

2 many times they have afflicted me from my youth, yet they have not prevailed against me.

3 Even though the ploughmen plow my back. They make their furrows long.

4 Lord, You are righteous. You cut apart the cords of the wicked that bind me; You free me.

5 You disappoint and turn back all those who hate me.

6 You make them be as the grass on the housetops, which withers before it grows up;

7 neither the reaper nor sheave binder fill their hand with it.

8 Those who go by them do not say, "The blessing of the Lord be on you", or "we bless you in God's name."

PP 130

1 Out of the depths I cry to You, Lord.

2 You hear my voice. Your ears are attentive to the voice of my petitions.

3 You do not keep a record of sins or I could not stand before You.

4 But You forgive me, and I fear You.

5 I wait for You, Lord. My soul waits. My hope is in Your word.

6 My soul longs for You more than watchmen long for the morning.

7 Lord, I hope in You, for with You, there is loving kindness. Abundant redemption is with You.

8 You redeem me from all my sins.

PP 131

1 Lord, my heart is not arrogant, nor my eyes proud. I do not concern myself with great matters, or things too wonderful for me.

2 I have stilled and quieted my soul, like a weaned child with his mother, like a weaned child is my soul within me.

3 My hope is in You, Lord, from this time forward and forever more.

1 Lord, You remember me and all my affliction.

2 You remember how David swore to You, and vowed to You, the Mighty One of Jacob:

3 "Surely I will not go into my house, nor go up onto my bed;

4 I will not give sleep to my eyes, or slumber to my eyelids,

5 until I find out a place for You, a dwelling for You, the Mighty One of Jacob."

6 "Behold, I heard of it in Ephrathah. I found it in the field of Jaar."

7 "I will go into Your dwelling place. I will worship at Your footstool."

8 Lord, You arise, coming into Your resting place; You, and the ark of Your strength.

9 Your priests are clothed with righteousness. Your saints shout for joy!

10 For Your servant David's sake, You do not turn away the face of Your anointed one.

11 You have sworn to David in truth. You will not turn from it: "I will set the fruit of your body on your throne.

12 If your children will keep My covenant, My testimony that I will teach them, their children also will sit on your throne forever more."

13 For You, God, have chosen Zion. You have desired it for Your habitation, saying,

14 "This is My resting place forever. I will live here, for I have desired it.

15 I will abundantly bless her provision. I will satisfy her poor with bread.

16 I will also clothe her priests with salvation. Her saints will shout aloud for joy.

17 I will make the horn of David to bud there. I have ordained a lamp for My anointed.

18 I will clothe his enemies with shame, but on David's head, his crown will shine."

PP 133 PP 133

1 See how good and how pleasant it is for brothers to live together in unity!

2 It is like precious oil on the head, that runs down on the beard, even Aaron's beard, that comes down on the edge of his robes,

3 like the dew of Hermon, that comes down on the hills of Zion; for there, You, Lord, give Your blessing, even life forever more.

PP 134

1 Lord, I praise You, along with all Your servants; even those who stand by night in Your house!

2 I lift up my hands in the sanctuary in praise to You!

3 You bless me from Zion, even You who made heaven and earth.

 PP 135

1 I praise You, God! I praise Your name! With all who are Your servants, I praise You.

2 I stand in Your house; in the courts of Your house.

3 God, I praise You, for You are good. I sing praises to Your name, for that is pleasant.

4 You chose Jacob for Yourself; Israel for Your own possession.

5 I know that You are great; that You are above all gods.

6 Whatever pleases You, that is what You do, in heaven and on earth, in the seas throughout their depths.

7 You cause the clouds to rise from the ends of the earth. You make lightnings with the rain. You bring the wind out of Your treasuries.

8 You struck the firstborn of Egypt, both of man and animal.

9 You sent signs and wonders into the middle of Egypt, on Pharaoh, and on all his servants.

10 You struck many nations, and killed mighty kings—

11 Sihon king of the Amorites, Og king of Bashan, and all the kingdoms of Canaan—

12 and gave their land as a possession to Israel, Your people.

13 Your name, Lord, endures forever; Your renown, Lord, throughout all generations.

14 For You judge Your people and have compassion on Your servants, of whom I am one.

15 The idols of the nations are silver and gold, the work of men's hands.

16 They have mouths, but they cannot speak. They have eyes, but they cannot see.

17 They have ears, but they cannot hear, neither is there any breath in their mouths.

18 Those who make them are like them; yes, everyone who trusts in them.

19 I praise You, Lord! Along with the house of Israel and the house of Aaron, I praise You!

20 I praise You, Lord! Along with the house of Levi and all who fear You, I praise You!

21 Blessed are You, Lord, from Zion, who dwells in Jerusalem. I praise You!

1 Lord, I give You thanks, for You are good. Your loving kindness endures forever.

2 I give You thanks, God of gods, for Your loving kindness endures forever.

3 I give You thanks, Lord of lords, for Your loving kindness endures forever.

4 I give thanks to You, alone, because You do great wonders. Your loving kindness endures forever.

5 I give thanks to You, who by Your understanding made the heavens, for Your loving kindness endures forever.

6 I give thanks to You, who spread out the earth above the waters, for Your loving kindness endures forever.

7 I give thanks to You, who made the great lights, for Your loving kindness endures forever;

8 the sun to rule by day, for Your loving kindness endures forever;

9 the moon and stars to rule by night, for Your loving kindness endures forever.

10 I give thanks to You, who struck down the Egyptian firstborn, for Your loving kindness endures forever.

11 I give thanks to You, who brought out Israel from among the Egyptians, for Your loving kindness endures forever;

12 with a strong hand, and with an outstretched arm, for Your loving kindness endures forever.

13 I give thanks to You, who divided the Red Sea, for Your loving kindness endures forever;

14 and made Israel to pass through the middle of it, for Your loving kindness endures forever.

15 But You overthrew Pharaoh and his army in the Red Sea, for Your loving kindness endures forever.

16 I give thanks to You, who led Your people through the wilderness, for Your loving kindness endures forever.

17 I give thanks to You, who destroyed great kings, for Your loving kindness endures forever.

18 You killed mighty kings, for Your loving kindness endures forever;

19 Sihon king of the Amorites, for Your loving kindness endures forever;

20 Og king of Bashan, for Your loving kindness endures forever.

21 You gave their land as a possession to Your people, for Your loving kindness endures forever;

22 even a heritage to Israel, Your servant, for Your loving kindness endures forever.

23 You remember us in our low estate, for Your loving kindness endures forever;

24 and deliver us from our adversaries, for Your loving kindness endures forever.

25 You give food to every creature, for Your loving kindness endures forever.

26 I give thanks to You, the God of heaven, for Your loving kindness endures forever.

PP 137

PP 137

1 By the rivers of Babylon, there we sat down. Yes, we wept, when we remembered Zion.

2 On the willows in that land, we hung up our harps.

3 For there, those who led us captive asked us for songs. Those who tormented us demanded songs of joy: "Sing us one of the songs of Zion!"

4 Lord, how can we sing Your song in a foreign land?

5 If I forget you, Jerusalem, let my right hand forget its skill.

6 Let my tongue stick to the roof of my mouth if I do not remember you; if I do not prefer Jerusalem above my chief joy.

7 Lord, You remember that the children of Edom, in the day of Jerusalem's destruction, said, "Destroy it! Destroy it even to its foundation!"

8 The daughter of Babylon is doomed to destruction. Lord, You happily repay them for what they have done to us.

9 You are happy as You cause their little ones to be dashed against the rock.

1 Lord, I give You thanks with my whole heart. Before the gods, I sing praises to You.

2 I bow down toward Your holy temple and give thanks to Your name for Your loving kindness and for Your truth. You exalt Your name and Your word above all.

3 In the day that I call, You answer me. You encourage me with strength in my soul.

4 All the kings of the earth give You thanks, Lord, for they hear the words of Your mouth.

5 Yes, they sing of Your ways for Your glory is great!

6 For though You are enthroned on high, You look after the lowly; but You know the proud from afar.

7 Though I walk in the middle of trouble, You save me. You stretch out Your hand against the wrath of my enemies. Your right hand saves me.

8 Lord, You complete that which concerns me. Your loving kindness endures forever. You do not forsake the works of Your own hands.

1 Lord, You search me, and You know me.

2 You know my sitting down and my rising up. You perceive my thoughts from afar.

3 You search out my path and my lying down, and You are acquainted with all my ways.

4 Before I speak a word, Lord, You know it altogether.

5 You hem me in behind and before. You lay Your hand on me.

6 This knowledge of You is beyond me. It is too lofty for me. I cannot attain it.

7 Where could I go from Your Spirit? Or where could I flee from Your presence?

8 If I ascend up into heaven, You are there. If I make my bed in the deep, You are there!

9 If I take the wings of the dawn and settle in the uttermost parts of the sea,

10 even there Your hand leads me, and Your right hand holds me.

11 If I say, "Surely the darkness surrounds me and the light around me is like the night,"

12 even the darkness is not dark to You, but the night shines like the day. The darkness is like light to You.

13 For You formed my inmost being. You knit me together in my mother's womb.

14 I give You thanks for I am fearfully and wonderfully made. Your works are wonderful. My soul knows that very well.

15 My frame was not hidden from You, when I was made in secret, woven together in the depths of the earth.

16 Your eyes saw my body before You formed me. In Your book, You wrote all my days before a single one came to be; all the days that You ordained for me.

17 How precious to me are Your thoughts, God! How vast is their sum!

18 If I would count them, they are more in number than the grains of sand. When I wake up, I am still with You.

19 God, You kill the wicked. You send away from me the bloodthirsty men!

20 For they speak against You wickedly. Your enemies take Your name in vain.

21 Lord, I hate those who hate You. I am grieved with those who rise up against You.

22 I hate them with perfect hatred. They are my enemies.

23 You search me, God, and You know my heart. You try me and You know my thoughts.

24 You see if there is any wicked way in me, and You lead me in the everlasting way.

PP 140 PP 140

1 Lord, You deliver me from evil men. You preserve me from violent men;

2 those who devise mischief in their hearts. They continually gather themselves together for war.

3 They have sharpened their tongues like a serpent. Viper's poison is on their lips.

4 Lord, You keep me from the hands of the wicked. You preserve me from the violent men who are determined to trip my feet.

5 The proud hide a snare for me. They spread the cords of a net by the path. They set traps for me.

6 I say to You, "You are my God." You listen to the cry of my petitions.

7 You, the Lord, the strength of my salvation, cover my head in the day of battle.

8 You do not grant the desires of the wicked. You do not let their evil plans succeed or they would become proud.

9 You make the mischief of their own lips cover the heads of those who surround me.

10 You make burning coals fall on them. You throw them into the fire, into miry pits, from where they never rise.

11 An evil speaker is not established in the earth. Destruction hunts the violent man to overthrow him.

12 Lord, I know that You maintain my cause because I am afflicted. You give me justice because I am needy.

13 I give thanks to Your name because I am righteous. I dwell in Your presence because I am upright.

1 Lord, I call on You, and You come to me quickly! You listen to my voice when I call to You.

2 My prayer comes before You like incense; the lifting up of my hands like the evening sacrifice.

3 Lord, You set a watch before my mouth. You guard the door of my lips.

4 I do not incline my heart to any evil thing, nor practice deeds of wickedness with evil men. I do not eat of their delicacies.

5 When the righteous strike me, it is a kindness to me; when he reproves me, it is like oil on my head. My head does not refuse it. My prayer is always against evildoer's deeds whose

6 judges are thrown down from the rocks. The wicked hear and learn from my words, for they are well spoken.

7 They say, "As when one plows and breaks up the earth, our bones are scattered at the mouth of the grave."

8 My eyes are on You, God, my Lord. I take refuge in You. You do not let my soul go down to the grave.

9 You keep me from the snare which they laid for me; from the traps of my enemies.

10 You cause all the wicked to fall together into their own nets while I pass safely by.

PP 142

1 Lord, I cry with my voice to You. With my voice, I ask You for mercy.

2 I pour out my complaint before You. I tell You my troubles.

3 When my spirit is overwhelmed within me, You know the route that I take. On the path in which I walk, my enemies hide a snare for me.

4 You look on my right and see; for there is no one who is concerned for me. There is no refuge for me. No one cares for my soul.

5 But, Lord, I cry to You and I say, "You are my refuge, my portion in the land of the living."

6 You listen to my cry, for I am in desperate need. You deliver me from my persecutors, for they are too strong for me.

7 You bring my soul out of prison and I give You praise. The righteous surround me, for You are good to me.

PP 143

1 You hear my prayer, Lord. You listen to my petitions. In Your faithfulness and righteousness, You give me relief.

2 You do not bring judgment on me, Your servant, even though, in Your sight, no man living is righteous, without You.

226

3 My enemy pursues my soul. He strikes my life down to the ground. He makes me live in dark places, as those who have been long dead.

4 Therefore my spirit is overwhelmed within me. My heart within me is discouraged.

5 I remember the days of old. I meditate on all Your works. I contemplate the work of Your hands.

6 I spread out my hands to You. My soul thirsts for You, like a parched land.

7 Behold, You hurry to answer me, Lord. When my spirit fails, You do not hide Your face from me. Therefore, I do not become like those who go down into the pit.

8 You cause me to hear Your loving kindness in the morning, for I trust in You. You show me the way in which to walk, for I lift up my soul to You.

9 You deliver me from my enemies. I flee to You and You hide me.

10 You teach me to do Your will, for You are my God. Your Spirit is good. You lead me in the land of uprightness.

11 You save me, Lord, for Your name's sake. In Your righteousness, You bring my soul out of trouble.

12 In Your loving kindness, You cut off my enemies and destroy all those who afflict my soul, for I am Your servant.

PP 144

1 I bless You, Lord, my rock, who trains my hands for war, and my fingers for battle.

2 You are my loving kindness, my fortress, my high tower, my deliverer, my shield, and my God in whom I take refuge, for You subdue people under me.

3 Lord, what is man, that You care for him? Or the son of man, that You think of him?

4 Like all men, I am just a breath. My days are like a shadow that passes away.

5 You part Your heavens and come down. You touch the mountains and they smoke.

6 You throw out lightning and scatter my enemies. You send out Your arrows and rout them.

7 You stretch out Your hand from above, rescue me, and deliver me out of strong waters; out of the hands of my enemies,

8 whose mouths speak deceit, and whose right hand is a right hand of lies.

9 I sing a new song to You, God. On a ten-stringed lyre, I sing praises to You.

10 You give salvation to kings; You rescued David, Your servant, from the deadly sword.

11 You also rescue me, and deliver me out of the hands of my enemies, whose mouths speak deceit, whose right hand is a right hand of lies.

12 Then You make my sons like well-nurtured plants and my daughters like pillars carved to adorn a palace.

13 My barns are full, filled with all kinds of provision. My sheep produce thousands, and tens of thousands, in my fields.

14 My oxen pull heavy loads. There is no breaking through my walls, no going away into slavery, and no outcry of anguish in my streets.

15 Happy am I, with all the people who are in such a situation. Happy am I, with all the people whose God is You, Lord.

PP 145 PP 145

1 I exalt You, my God, the King. I praise Your name forever and ever.

2 Every day I praise You. I extol Your name forever and ever.

3 Great are You, Lord, and greatly to be praised! Your greatness is unsearchable.

4 One generation commends Your works to another and declares Your mighty acts.

5 I meditate on the glorious majesty of Your honor, and on Your wondrous works.

6 Men speak of the might of Your awesome acts. I declare Your greatness.

7 I rejoice in the memory of Your great goodness and sing of Your righteousness.

8 Lord, You are gracious, merciful, slow to anger, and of great loving kindness.

9 You are good to all. Your tender mercies are over all Your works.

10 All Your works praise You, Lord. Your saints extol You.

11 I speak of the glory of Your kingdom and talk about Your power,

12 to make known to all the sons of men Your mighty acts and the glory of the majesty of Your kingdom.

13 Your kingdom is an everlasting kingdom. Your dominion endures throughout all generations. You are faithful in all Your words and loving in all Your deeds.

14 You lift up all who fall and raise up all those who are bowed down.

15 All eyes wait for You. You give them their food in due season.

16 You open Your hand and satisfy the desire of every living thing.

17 Lord, You are righteous in all Your ways and gracious in all Your works.

18 You are near to me and to all those who call on You; to all who call on You in truth.

19 You fulfill my desires, and the desires of all who fear You. You also hear my cry, and You save me.

20 You preserve me, along with all who love You, but You destroy all the wicked.

21 My mouth speaks Your praises, Lord. All flesh blesses Your holy name forever and ever.

PP 146 PP 146

1 Lord, I praise You! My soul praises You.

2 While I live, I praise You. I sing praises to You, my God, as long as I live.

3 I do not put my trust in princes; in man who has no power to save me.

4 His spirit departs, and he returns to the earth. In that very day, his thoughts perish.

5 Blessed am I because I have You, the God of Jacob, for my help. My hope is in You, my God,

6 who made heaven and earth, the sea, and all that is in them. You are faithful forever.

7 You execute justice for me because I am oppressed. You give me food because I am hungry. You free me because I am a prisoner.

8 Lord, You open my eyes because I am blind. You raise me up because I am bowed down. You love me because I am righteous in Your sight.

9 You preserve the foreigners. You uphold the fatherless and the widow, but You turn the way of the wicked upside down.

10 Lord, You will reign forever; the God of Zion, to all generations. I praise You!

PP 147 PP 147

1 Lord, I praise You for it is good to sing praises to You, my God; for it is pleasant and fitting to praise You.

2 You build up Jerusalem. You gather me together with the outcasts of Israel.

3 You heal me with those who are broken-hearted and bind up my wounds.

4 You count the number of the stars. You call them all by their names.

5 Great are You, Lord, and mighty in power. Your understanding is infinite.

6 You uphold me because I am humble, but You bring the wicked down to the ground.

7 I sing to You with thanksgiving. I sing Your praises on the harp.

8 You cover the sky with clouds and prepare rain for the earth. You make grass grow on the mountains.

9 You provide food for the livestock, and for the young ravens when they call.

10 You do not delight in the strength of the horse. You take no pleasure in the legs of a man.

11 You take pleasure in me because I fear You, along with all who fear You; because I hope in Your loving kindness.

12 Jerusalem praises You! Zion praises You, God!

13 For You strengthen the bars of her gates. You bless her children within her.

14 You make peace in her borders. You fill her with the finest wheat.

15 You send out Your commandment to the earth. Your word runs very swiftly.

16 You give snow like wool, and scatter frost like ashes.

17 You hurl down Your hail like pebbles. No one can stand before Your cold blast.

18 You send out Your word and melt them. You cause Your wind to blow, and the waters flow.

19 You show Your word to Jacob; Your statutes and Your ordinances to Israel.

20 You have not done this for any other nation. Other nations do not know Your ordinances. I praise You!

PP 148 PP 148

1 Lord, I praise You! The heavens praise You! They praise You in the heavenly heights!

2 All Your angels and Your heavenly armies praise You!

3 The sun, the moon, and all Your shining stars praise You!

4 The heavens of heavens, and waters that are above the heavens praise You.

5 They all praise Your name, for You commanded and created them all.

6 You established them forever and ever. You made a decree which will not pass away.

7 The great sea creatures, and all the ocean depths praise You from the earth.

8 Lightning and hail, snow and clouds, stormy winds, all obey Your commands.

9 Mountains and all hills, fruit trees and all cedars,

10 wild animals and all livestock, small creatures and flying birds,

11 kings of the earth and all peoples, princes and all judges of the earth,

12 both young men and maidens, old men and children, all praise You.

13 They all praise Your name, for Your name alone is exalted. Your glory is above the earth and the heavens.

14 You lifted up the horn of Your people, the praise of all Your saints, even of the children of Israel, a people near to You. I praise You!

1 Lord, I praise You! I sing to You a new song; Your praise in the assembly of the saints.

2 With all of Israel, I rejoice in You who made us. The children of Zion are joyful in You, their King.

3 With Israel, I praise Your name in the dance! I sing praises to You with tambourine and harp!

4 For You, Lord, take pleasure in Your people, of whom I am one. You crown me with salvation because I am humble.

5 With all Your saints, I rejoice in this honor. I sing for joy on my bed.

6 Your high praises are in my mouth, and a two-edged sword is in my hand,

7 to execute vengeance on the nations, and punishment on the peoples;

8 to bind their kings with chains, and their nobles with fetters of iron;

9 to execute on them Your written judgment. All Your saints, of whom I am one, have this honor. I praise You!

1 Lord, I praise You! I praise You in Your sanctuary! I praise You in Your heavens for Your acts of power!

2 I praise You for Your mighty acts! I praise You according to Your excellent greatness!

3 I praise You with the sounding of the trumpet! I praise You with harp and lyre!

4 I praise You with tambourine and dancing! I praise You with stringed instruments and flute!

5 I praise You with loud cymbals! I praise You with resounding cymbals!

6 Everything that has breath praises, You, Lord! I praise You!

www.personalpsalms.com

Made in the USA
Columbia, SC
01 November 2024

45462911R00133